I want to ski

Paul R. Williamson

ACKNOWLEDGMENTS

My artistic friend Frances Coleman for all the sketches, including the cover sketch.

My son Andrew and his wife Julia for their endless patience answering all my IT questions, and other procedure problems.

ISBN-10: 146816533X

ISBN-13: 9781468165333

CONTENTS

1 CONTEMPLATING SKIING

(Everything written in italics between brackets are in general just comments which I have added in the hope that it will help to you, and is generally only for your interest, rather than being essential information that you need to learn)

I hope this book will be of interest to all skiers, although the people I particularly had in mind when I started writing were the people, mostly adults, who have problems and need some help learning how to ski, as well as beginners. From experience and from conversations I've had with people I have met while skiing, I have concluded that there are a lot of people like myself, who need to understand "why" or more accurately, the "reasons why". That is, they need to know the reason why they have to lean forwards and or downhill and why they need to transfer their weight et cetera, in other words they need to know the fundamental principles and theories involved in skiing, rather than just simply being told to do this and that or the other, which are just the mechanics of "how" to ski, if they are going to have any confidence in what they are doing when they try to put "how to ski" into practice. To put it another way, these are the people who have problems if they are only told "how" to do things, when what they really need to know is the "reasons why", because otherwise they will not have any confidence in what they are trying to do on skis, and without any confidence there is not much chance of them succeeding. Therefore as well as the "how", I intend to explain the reasons why and also give you my theories and the logic behind my theories, as well as explaining the principles and mechanics of how to ski.

Let me put it another way, I believe the main reason for a lot of people's difficulties is that it is necessary for them to know "why" they have to follow the instructions given to them on how to ski, rather than only being taught just "how" to ski, which is not the same thing. As in my particular case and I suspect in many other peoples too, especially if they are adults trying to learn to ski, if it is not explained to them why you need to follow the instructions given to you to perform any operations, that is, why you have to lean forwards or why you need to have your weight on your lower ski et cetera, then it is highly unlikely you will have any confidence in what you are trying to do, and that means it is most unlikely that you will be able to succeed.

In my case I didn't start learning to ski until I was in my late twenties, so that made me an adult or mature student, I'm now in my seventies, and I have to admit that as keen as I was, I found it very difficult learning to ski. I honestly believe that if it had also been taught the reason "why" I needed to follow the instructions I was being given, that is, if I had been given the theory, or had the principles explained to me, then I think I would have been a lot quicker at learning how to ski.

For people who have never been skiing, from observations and anecdotal evidence, I would guess of all the people taking their first skiing holiday, that something like about a quarter of them will give up and make it their last, about half will vary from becoming relatively accomplished to the natural sportsman or woman, who seem to be instinctively able to learn how to ski with little more than a bit of basic instruction. I've even known people to claim they needed no instruction at all, but maybe they were not telling me the truth.

However, if it doesn't happen like that for you, then it indicates that you are in the other group which I think this book could help, who are keen and want to ski, but have difficulties. For those people who have problems learning how to ski and show very little promise, which included me when I first started when I was 28, but who are still enthusiastic and determined, and are probably the people who don't have a natural aptitude for skiing and consequently need all the help they can get, including all the details on why as well as how to ski being explained to them. These are also the people who will normally be taking a one or two weeks skiing holiday each year and who are commonly known as "piste bashers" because, until they have become fully accomplished skiers, if they have any sense, they will stick to skiing on the piste and not "off piste", well not intentionally anyway, and of course I would also like to think this book will be of interest to anyone else who skis.

Right, from now on in this and the next chapter I shall be talking about things like clothing, or picking out a resort for a holiday, therefore people who have already been skiing and don't need any further introduction to skiing, and want to get on with reading about how to actually ski, they can now skip directly to page 17.

Most people find if they join a ski school and they are put in a class that's about the same skiing standard as they are, that it's a lot of fun; and anyway, if you find that you are not happy with the class you have been allocated, it shouldn't be any problem to get it changed. When I started of course I attended ski school classes and I even had some private tuition.

Once you have learned to ski well enough so that you can venture away from the nursery slopes, I think it is always sensible if you are not in a ski class with an instructor, to a least have an accomplished skier with you, not just to help you to learn how to ski, but for all sorts of safety reasons. Skiing is a dangerous sport, not only to yourself, but to anyone else in your vicinity, more especially when you loose control of your skiing. Also for beginners there is the serious risk of getting lost or by mistake finding yourself on a too difficult piste, it will happen to you all too frequently even when you have learnt to ski well enough to venture out on your own.

I believe one of the problems with skiing instructors, who have probably been skiing ever since kindergarten and are what I would normally term as being "natural skiers", that is, they don't have to think about what they are doing any more than we do about how to walk, even though we had to learn how to walk when we were toddlers. It's just that I think they have no idea of the problems us poor beginners, especially "adult" beginners have when our only previous knowledge of skiing has probably been acquired from watching the TV or films. Well, that's my theory for what it's worth!

In my case as I have already indicated, I reckon that part of my particular problem was that I needed to know "why", rather than just how to do different things, so as to have the confidence that I needed to be able to learn to ski, or I imagine do anything else. I suppose it's just the way my brain works, anyway the trouble was at ski school I was not being taught "why", but only that that is what I had to do, or to put it another way, I was told that if I did this that or the other I would be able to ski without explaining why, but I'm afraid that didn't work for me. So after many skiing holidays, I concluded I knew the ski teachers script on how to ski as well as they did, and there was not a lot more I was going to learn in ski school to improve my skiing, and so I decided I needed to try a new tack.

I took to observing other people who looked like good skiers, and try to copy what I saw them doing, and see how I got on that way. Looking back, I would say that for me it seems to have worked quite well, I took to watching skiers while I was taking a break at any piste side restaurant. I would try to pick out how the good skiers moved and any other tips that I could pick out and then try to emulate them. Funnily enough though, watching the poorer skiers making their mistakes seemed to be even more edifying than watching the good skiers, because it helped me to realise what was the cause of me making my mistakes. So there you are, between watching and trying and tips I picked up from other people around the bars and things I just discovered, more often than not by accident or by trial and error, that after years of perseverance and dogged determination I now reckon I've eventually got the hang of it. After that, all I needed to do to write this book was to work out the "why", or in other words the principles and theory. I know this is not the normal sequence for learning how to ski, or to learn anything else for that matter. Never mind, because for you, you can now do it the proper way round by first reading this book to learn the principles and the theories in the comfort of your arm chair if you so wish, before even starting out on skis.

I don't think there can be a problem that any adult person learning to ski has faced that I am not familiar with, as opposed to the average ski instructor, who probably learnt to ski in his romper suit and will probably only know what difficulties adults have from what they have been told by their pupils. I don't want you to think I'm knocking ski instructors, generally they do a fine job, it's just that I think theirs, and my experiences are different.

I therefore thought it would be a good idea not to waste all this hard earned knowledge, but instead, write it down for the benefit of other people behind me, so that they can avoid struggle in my wake. I accept that this may be an unconventional way to claim to have the authority to write a book on how to learn to ski, never the less, I believe it works well enough.

Without wanting to be over dramatic, I believe my experience gives me a unique insight into the problems that the quarter or so of beginners have, who are determined but show very little promise. In fact I think it would be fair to say that my expertise comes from quite the opposite direction to that of any ski instructor, as what I think sets me apart from the ski instructor is that a lot of the professional ski instructors, who can ski simply by instinct, don't understand the difficulties us poor adult beginners have, trying to arrange the bits and pieces of our body so as to be able to make the manoeuvres that are required of us. Regarding children, who's bodies are so supple they seem to be able to pick up how to ski quite effortlessly and should therefore be considered for future ski instructor material.

Of course I have many excuses for all the problems I had, and for showing very little promise, which I am only too happy to share with you as I think you may find them interesting, but because of the progress skiing has made since 1963 when I started, in the days of leather boots with laces and wooden skis, I don't think that these excuses can be used now.

For a start, whether you were a beginner or an expert, the same system was used to measure you for the length of your skis. You were asked to raise an arm above your head and were then given skis that reached up to about your wrist, which for me was 205-210 cms, I am 6 ft 1inch tall and that reached some 25 cms above the top of my head and believe me I now know that didn't help. I would have stood a far better chance of learning how to ski if I had been given skis, well to start with about 170 cms long or even less, but in those days I didn't know that, and anyway with such short skis I would have been the laughing stock of the resort. It was the macho thing in those days to use long skis, as it was assumed that the longer they where, then the better skier you must be. Skiers egos!

Another thing I remember was that the instructors I had in my beginners class, instructed us to lean out when making a turn, when what I think they really meant was for us to put our weight on the outside ski, and I guess like many other beginners, I struggled for years leaning out when trying to make a turn, before I twigged that mistake. I even had an instructor once who would actually bend at his waist to look as though he was leaning out when he demonstrated the turn to us. I really don't know why, maybe he thought he was demonstrating to us the best way to learn to make a turn, but looking back on it, frankly it's a complete mystery to me what he was trying to do, or for that matter, how the idea of leaning out when making a turn got started, in fact if anything, you need to lean into the turn, but essentially, with your weight on your outside ski.

Instead of the old double leather skiing boots, we now wear the modern plastic ski boots that give you a lot more support, reaching high up above your ankles so that your ankles are virtually clamped into the correct position whether you like it or not, so that's another problem solved.

Actually I have a soft spot for the old double leather boots, the inner boot was made of soft leather, which was very comfortable and the outer boot was made of very stiff leather, so as to give your ankles support. When you were not skiing, you simply eased off the laces of the outer boot and then they were perfectly comfortable to walk around in, or to even to go dancing if you so wished.

The 5 o'clock hop was a regular thing in those days, still in our ski boots, that is, until a dance floor collapsed at a resort where they were dancing the Madison. For anyone who doesn't know what the Madison dance is and frankly I only have a vague recollection myself, but I do remember that every so often you all had to give a hop in unison, that I imagine is when the floor gave way and so I guess, that was the reason for the end of the Madison at the 5 O'clock hop. Anyway, now-a-days nobody dances in their ski boots anymore.

When I started skiing, another thing they didn't have were mechanical piste groomers, piste maintenance was all done manually, which meant there were lots of humps and bumps on the pistes, not nicely groomed as they are today, I know at one resort, anyone volunteering to groom the piste had to arrive in time to start before 7.00 am. They then had to take a shovel and collect snow from off the piste to repair any bare patches, or if it had been snowing then they had to side step up the mountain to pack the new snow down. A lot of work for a little pay other than a day's ski pass and the results, well to be honest by today's standards left a lot to be desired, even allowing that ice was ice and there was not a lot they could do about that before they had mechanical groomers. Even us poor beginners had to step down any new snow fall with our skis, to make an area to practise our turns or what ever.

The original piste groomers were just a special type of "track laying" (*crawler*) tractors. Then rollers were attached at the rear so they became piste packers. Next a bulldozer like blade was fitted at the front to make them into piste groomers, so what's the betting that next they will be fitted with a fan so they will become piste stylist's. With the introduction of piste groomers it's now possible to maintain pistes better by removing any unwanted humps and bumps that might develop, which of course we used to have to negotiate, so that makes it a lot better for the blue piste skiers.

Well that's enough of my excuses, if I really wanted to I expect I could carry on and write the whole book about nothing else. I've been told, probably by my parents or maybe it was in my school report, that I had an excuse for every occasion and let me tell you that's not easy, it requires a lot of practice.

Let's carry on and think about what skiing involves for beginners. To learn to ski involves a lot of physical activity and can be hard work, so you will need to be reasonably athletic and fit, although I've got along well enough without being too athletic even though I consider myself to be reasonably fit, if you are out of condition, it could be a painful experience for you, but I'm sure if you keep persevering you will eventually overcome all such difficulties. The best suggestion I have for getting fit for skiing is to take to riding a bicycle, or on an exercise bike, as it will exercise all the muscles that you use the most when you ski. For younger people it shouldn't cause any insurmountable problems, but for older people it will be more of a challenge, but I've met many people who didn't start skiing until after they were 50. I even met two farmers from Kent on the snow train, who claimed they didn't start skiing until they were over 60, I don't know what their standard of skiing was, but who cares, they seemed to have enjoyed themselves. Come to think of it, I am not so sure that they might have been pulling my leg, because I grew up in a farming community, but not in Kent and I know some farmers have a very strange sense of humour.

If in spite of all I have said you are still determined to go skiing then your next concern will be clothing and choosing a resort.

2 SKI HOLIDAY PREPARATIONS

Because ski resorts are normally high up, on a bright sunny day in the still dry air with clear blue skies you can feel really warm, even though the air temperature is well below freezing. You may even choose to stop off at a mountain restaurant, as we did in a beginners class I was in once and strip off to our waist so as to have a chance to show off our beautiful white pallid bodies and do some sunbathing, while supping a nice glass of beer, which must have been one hell of a sight for sore eyes. We stood our skis in the snow to hang our clothes on and it was all very pleasant until it was time for us to carry on skiing. It was only when we went to put our clothes back on that we discovered our sweat had turned into ice, so that they were frozen stiff. However, once we got our clothes on, what with the hopping and jumping around the ice didn't last long, but it just demonstrates what the difference being up a mountain makes. Tell me how many people do you see outside sunbathing in England in the middle of winter when it's freezing? Of course the women, bless their little cotton socks thought it was all very hilarious, as in those days they didn't strip to the waist to sun bath when they where in a beginners class, or at least not while I was around.

Clothing.

If you have decided that you intend to give skiing a go, then it's now necessary to start getting serious. In spite of my remark about sun bathing when it's been freezing, it only needs a slight breeze to change that situation. It is essential when skiing to keep warm, especially for beginners, who may have to stand around a lot when in ski classes on a dull day. In fact I would be prepared to go so far as to say that "not" keeping warm will seriously hinder your ability to learn to ski, because it will reduce the efficiency of your muscles. If necessary then disregard fashion, being fashionable while you keep warm is quiet commendable, but it is not acceptable if you do not keep warm, just to be fashionable. So unless you want to cripple your self, getting cold is absolutely not recommended for skiing.

As skiing is a physically active sport, your muscles need to be warm to operate safely, efficiently and for you to be comfortable. If your muscles are cold they will tire quickly and you will seriously increase the risk of damaging them, maybe causing you to have an accident, like pulling a ligament, which will take a long time to get better, apart from being very painful, and it is quite likely that it can completely spoil your holiday.

Therefore when skiing, it is necessary to have the proper clothing, especially the outer clothing, which may consist of ski trousers or salepets (*which are like well padded overalls but with style*) and an anorak, or alternatively, an all in one ski-suit (*which is like a stylish well padded boiler suit*). I don't think beginners should think of wearing any other sort of clothing. Occasionally you may see experienced skiers wearing jeans or anything else they fancy but although it will be a mystery to me, we may assumed they know what they are doing. All things being equal, the all in one ski-suit is the warmest, but if suddenly the sun comes out and it gets too warm, you may wish you had an anorak which can be removed or be opened to allow air to flow around you so you don't overheat. For that reason I personally prefer an anorak and salepets or sometimes in the warmer springtime, ski trousers. Whatever you chose, it is essential that it is made of a water proof and porous or breathable material, otherwise, because of the freezing air making the outside clothing material very cold, your sweat will condense inside your clothing and make your underclothes wet, uncomfortable and you will very quickly get cold, I know this from experience. Now-a-days I would expect all clothing specially made for skiing to be made of breathable material.

Also I always insist when buying an anorak that it is fitted with a light-weight hood, which is normally stowed away in the collar. It is very useful if it starts snowing to protect you from any snow getting down your neck and melting, especially when the wind is blowing.

What under clothes you wear is your personal choice, but as I have said, it is essential that you keep warm, but at the same time try to avoid getting too hot or cold. A lot of people will tell you that it is better to wear two light weight jumpers instead of one heavy jumper, which gives you the option of taking one off if you get too warm and you can't argue with that. But when I tried two light weight jumpers instead of my usual heavy jumper, presumably because of the materials they were made of, they both rode-up my body and finished up under my armpits, which was not very comfortable and for me it was certainly not better than one heavy jumper. So there you are, for skiers, even putting on jumpers is not as simple as you might think. I normally pack at least two jumpers and probably three of different warmth and choose the one that I anticipate will be correct for the day's skiing. I've never regretted always packing a pair of Long Johns for when the weather turns really cold. I have been told that men can benefit from wearing a pair of ladies tights to keep them warm, but if you do for goodness sake don't mention it down at the pub.

There are other essential items you must have before you venture out on to the piste. You must have a pair of proper skiing gloves or mittens to protect your hands and keep them warm, ordinary gloves will not stay dry or be able to stand up to the wear and tear inflicted on them especially by beginners. I know because I tried and in no time at all, the gloves were soaking wet and completely ruined, not to mention that my hands were also freezing cold.

Finally, what to wear on your head? Skiers have earned a splendid reputation for wearing eccentric, unique and exotic hats, like Court Jester's and Clown's hats sometimes with ding-a-ling bells on, Slouch hats, Broad brimmed hats complete with dangling corks to keep non existent flies away, Bird's head hats with beaks and floppy wings, Panama hats and anything else in between ad infinitum have all been seen on the piste, to say nothing of the normal woolly bobble hats. However, there is a serious point that needs to made which is that as heat rises, you can lose up to half your body heat through your head, so in cold weather you need to wear a warm hat, and if you wear a woolly bobble hat and you get too hot, it is easy enough to take off and put it in your pocket.

In recent years helmets have appeared on the pistes, and for children in some ski schools I believe it's compulsory, I must admit that there have been occasions when I might have benefited from wearing one, fortunately I have been lucky and managed to get away without suffering any injury when losing control and falling when travelling at speed, miraculously missing rocks and trees I know not how, even now I don't like to think about it. I have to admit that now-a-days my progress is probably too sedate to require me to need to wear a helmet, it's the old arthritis you know.

Due to the strong sun's rays and the thinner atmosphere at higher altitudes, in addition to the reflection of the sun off the snow, you will need to protect your eyes with either sunglasses or goggles from getting "sun-blink". If you fail to protect your eyes and you start to suffer from sun-blink, I can assure you it is very painful and can even cause temporary blindness. Also due to the higher altitude, although it is wintertime, you will need to use a good sun cream for protection from not only the direct strong sun's rays but also from the rays reflected off the snow. Make a special point of protecting the top of your nose, I didn't and developed a persistent scab which at first I didn't bother too much about, until I eventually got round to seeing the doctor. He told me it was a skin cancer and also that there are a mass of nerves running up my nose which would have caused me some serious problems if I hadn't had the cancer treated, mind you I did not know until then that it was a cancer, anyway you have now been warned.

Because most of the time while you are skiing, you will be at higher altitudes than you are used to, you will therefore be in a lighter atmosphere, and as a result of the adiabatic lapse rate, especially as the air is normally dry, more often than not, although you may not realise it, the air temperature will be well below freezing. You will find that these conditions sap the energy of most short-term holiday skiers not used to high altitudes, so they will quickly feel more tired than they would at home, although this should not affect the younger twenty or thirty something year olds too much. In passing I should also mention that for much the same reasons, you can expect any cuts or other similar injuries, to take longer to heal.

Skiing Equipment

Now we come to your skiing equipment. I would recommend a first time skier or beginner, to start with opting to hire your skis and boots, which will be available in all resorts, as they are not cheap to buy. As a rule of thump a week's hire will cost roughly a 12th of their new price, bearing in mind that the life of a new pair of skis is probably no more than five years or so, depending on how well they have been maintained. Professionals probably renew their skis at least once, if not more often, every year, depending of the amount of wear they have had, but of course they get them at concessionary prices. As a beginner you only need to hire the standard skis and boots which will be easier to learn on, the superior boots are really intended for the better skiers and will basically be stiffer and less forgiving and are therefore unsuitable for beginners. Hiring the cheaper and more flexible standard skis, which could mean they are last seasons but will be perfectly adequate for beginners.

There are various types of ski boots depending on how they open up for you to put your feet in them, which may be fitted with this, that or the other feature that you may be impressed with, then go ahead and chose the ones that you prefer, but at the end of the day, once they are clipped up on your feet, as a beginner you won't know the difference as far as learning to ski is concerned. The important thing you must be sure of is that they fit correctly. Although they need to be close fitting so that your foot is held snugly but comfortably, they also need to be long enough so as not to cramp, chaff, or restrict your toes in any way, but neither too long, so as to be sure that your heel is held firmly in place. The buckles and straps that are used to tie-up your boot are adjustable so as to give the correct fitting round your ankles and over the top of your feet, so essentially it is the length and width of the boot that must be correct.

Once you have the ski boots that you have chosen clipped up, check that you can spread out your toes comfortably, that the width of the boot also fits comfortably, check that your heel is held firmly in place, as you do not want any looseness. Now try leaning forward without bending your knees so that your shins are pressing against the tongue of the boot and check again that your heels are held firmly and the rest of your foot is comfortable, walk around in them for a few minutes. If later you are not happy with them, then you can change them, "but" it is much better if you can get them right first time, if you don't and lets say they make your toes sore and they swell up, then it will be very difficult to try to change them for another pair that will fit your feet properly if you have swollen toes. So be patient but persistent to make sure your boots fit properly first time, if after that you are happy with them, there is not much more you can do to check that they are suitable for you, so you might as well take them.

Since I converted to skiing on parabolic or carving skis as they are now called, I have been hiring skis, which also saves me the bother of maintenance, storage and transport. Although they don't need to be as long as my old parallel skis, I am still working on the different ski lengths and at the same time it also allows me to choose a different length of ski for the prevailing conditions, so although it will be a little more expensive, one way and another there is a lot to be said for hiring skis if you are only going to take one or two weeks skiing holiday each year.

If after skiing for a few days you are sure that you will be taking up skiing as one of your life's pleasures, or if you are rich and just don't have to care about costs, then I recommend that the first piece of equipment you purchase is a pair of ski-boots, of course you must be sure that they fit you.

Having your own boots means that you can then be confident that on arrival, once you have got your skis, which shouldn't take long, even if you are hiring them, then you can start skiing right away, as unlike boots, it doesn't matter if you decide to change your skis as often as you like, and without causing you any problems, that is apart from annoying the hirer.

Ski poles are still simple to choose, any pole will do so long as the bottom of it's grip is level with your elbow when measured from the ground, or that your elbow is bent at right angles when you grip the ski pole and place the point on the ground, alternatively you can turn the ski pole up side down and hold the pole below it's basket (*the bit that stops it from going too deep into the snow*) to measure it's length more accurately. Should you ever reach the standard of a racer, then only your imagination is the limit as to how many wiggles you have in your ski-pole but otherwise, the standard straight pole will be perfectly fine for the ordinary piste bashers.

Choosing a Resort.

A few words for the first time skier on what alternative ways there are of going on a skiing holiday. First of all you can travel completely independently, I did when I started, the obvious advantages are the freedom of movement to wander from resort to resort as your fancy takes you, or for that matter if you are run out of town. If you are travelling alone or with just a friend it can be adventurous and a lot of fun, but also a bit chancy, you may also have some difficulty finding suitable accommodation, depending on how fussy you are. On more than one occasion I have finished up in the next village outside the ski resort, sometimes that led to finding a lot cheaper lodgings, so as they say, "there are swings and roundabouts", once I had to make do with sleeping in a straw loft over the cowshed for the night, but I'm sure there must be some regulation stopping farmers from doing that now-a-days. Price-wise, it will depend on your luck, but if you are looking for en-suite accommodation, it will normally cost you more than through a packaged holiday. Incidentally there is not much chance of finding casual accommodation in ski resorts in the French Alps during the high skiing season, where self catering apartments are more common, although you shouldn't have problems outside the resorts, I have normally been successful in the rest of the Alpine resorts. I soon realised that having a car was a great advantage, even though public transport was normally very good, except on Sundays. I say "was" because to be honest I haven't travelled independently for at least 15 or maybe even 20 years now, so I expect I might be a bit out of date.

I would consider it a major challenge to travel independently when you have family commitments. I found a reasonably satisfactory compromise, which was to just book your accommodation in advance, but that only allows you to be independent for journeying out and back. Even then, on one occasion the pension (*Guest house*) owner, who had told me he was happy if I went skiing on the morning of our departure, my wife and son didn't want to bother with a final ski, when I got back at about midday, I found we had been thrown out, and leaving me with an angry wife and an obstreperous child. The owner had dumped my clothes in my suitcase, he wouldn't even allow my wife any time to pack them properly for me, just because he had found another customer would you believe. I couldn't even have a shower or change my clothes until we booked into a hotel later for the night, but fortunately we where travelling by car.

Maybe a good idea might be for me to give you a brief resume of my introduction to skiing. At the time I was un-married and in my late 20's, when I had returned from abroad with some money in the bank and out of work, staying on my parent's farm in Norfolk in February. As I recall, it was when I realised that my father was eyeing me up for some work on the farm I started to think about taking a holiday, let me assure you that working on a farm in February in the nineteen sixties was not a lot of fun. My elder brother had already told me how much he had enjoyed skiing, so in February, that seemed like a good idea. All I knew about skiing was that you could ski in Austria, so I took some money out of the bank, packed a suitcase and went to London Victoria station. There I bought a ticket to Innsbruck and caught the train at about 3.00 pm as far as I can recall, which was due to arrive at Innsbruck via the Folkestone ferry, at about noon the following day but in fact it arrived at about 3.00 pm. Walking out of the station at Innsbruck I saw a English looking women with her leg in a plaster, we did not have global fashions in those days, other nations like the Austrians dressed differently to us, so I was able to concluded she must be an injured English skier. Her name was Rosemary and she turned out to be the representative for the ski club of Great Britain at a place called Igls, which in the early 1960's was very popular with the English. You could even buy that day's English newspaper at 9.00 am, anyway I joined Rosemary on the bus to go up to Igls so she could give me lots of useful advice on how to get started.

That night I splashed out on a posh hotel, which I felt I deserved after spending 24 hours or more on a train, possibly feeling tired and lazy also had something to do with it. The next day feeling bright eyed and bushy tailed, I set out to look for lodgings.

I was lucky enough to find a pension for about 12/6d or 62½p a night, bed and breakfast, including a boiled egg and a tot of Austrian brandy "to keep out the cold" according to the landlady. Bathing was an optional extra, available by arrangement at a near-by pension at 1½p per bath. After about a fortnight the dirty laundry in the cupboard disappeared and latter came back beautifully washed and ironed, and at no extra charge, which I put down to the landlady's commendable maternal instincts or maybe she just enjoyed doing washing and ironing. Those were the days.

It was not always like that, by contrast, a year or two later I was with some friends and we stayed at another pension where we were charged extra for everything, even for a tea bag when we wanted a second cup of tea, or for an extra portion of butter or jam, or a bread roll for breakfast. It's just the sort of "luck of the draw" when you go on an independent skiing holiday that makes it that much more interesting and it also gives you something to talk about in the pub when you get home. After all, it is most unlikely that anyone is going to believe any of your stories of "daring do" on or off the piste, whether they are true or not.

Back to Igls, having arranged my lodgings, I bought an anorak and a pair of skiing trousers (*not readily available in Norfolk in those days*), and then hired skis and boots. Now fully equipped except for ski-gloves, as I have already explained, I joined a beginner's class to launch myself into a sport that has never failed to afford me the greatest of pleasure.

Now-a-days, most people, including myself, either book a packaged skiing holiday, normally flying, it's convenient and usually good value for money. Personally, since I now live in Kent I've been using the snow train via Calais, (*which unfortunately has now been discontinued, although it is still available via Paris*) because you arrive at your resort in time to ski on the day of arrival, and you leave late enough to ski on the day of departure as well, giving you eight days skiing, instead of the usual six days, for a seven nights stay, although you have to leave home on the Friday afternoon and don't get back until Sunday morning. The snow train is probably more suitable for people living in the south east and London. It's also becoming quite common to book your holiday on line and drive out by car, especially for those who are taking a self-catering family holiday and want to take the kitchen sink with them. Then again, you may prefer booking your flight and accommodation and possibly car hire all on line.

On my first skiing holiday in Igls I met an Englishman who had driven out with his caravan, which he had intended to use as his accommodation, but apart from anything else, at night time it had turned out to be far too cold, which had caused him to retreat to a pension. I seem to remember he also had parking and other problems with the authorities. In those days caravans were only intended for summer holidays and the insulation was not so good, should the idea of using a caravan appeal to anyone now-a-days, I expect modern caravans are much better insulated.

Right, well that's the easy bit done.

3 GET READY TO START SKIING

Some basic information on starting to ski including the force of gravity & skiing etiquette.

When you have mastered all the information contained in this book, as I'm sure you will, according to my reckoning you will have become a very proficient skier, skiing like the naturally born expert skiers without giving it any more thought than you do about walking, as you stroll down the High Street.

I hope good skiers will also find this book worth reading, if only to help them to understand the problems us poor beginners especially adults may have learning to ski.

I'm afraid that it is necessary to take some time to explain some of the basic features that you need to know before we can start explaining how to ski. Put simply if anything about learning to ski can be put simple, there are two ways to ski, either using good techniques with skill, or alternatively, with just a bit of basic knowledge of how to ski and the use of brute force to achieve the rest of your aims. Of course while you are learning the skills and techniques to ski, you will probably have to augment your skiing by resorting to brute force. However, if you want to be able to ski comfortably, competently and without expending any unnecessary effort, then you can only do that if you have learnt and understood, and are able to put into practise the following required skiing skills and techniques, which you will also need to be able to do if you wish to carry on skiing as you get older and are less agile.

It is not my intention to make skiing sound difficult or for that matter highly technical, on the other hand it would be wrong of me to skimp or try to gloss over difficult explanations just for the sake of making skiing sound easy. At times I have given alternative explanations, so that one way or another I hope I will have catered for everyone. If on the other hand you still have difficulty understanding some of my explanations, it's probably not worth worrying too much about, as long as you are able to accept and understand the concept or idea, and then go out and try it in practise. After that, if you want, to you can always come back and check my explanations again later, to see if you can now make sense of it. Once you know and understand the basic principals of skiing and providing you keep your mind concentrated on what you are trying to do and start at the beginning, you should have no trouble learning how to ski, eventually maybe.

The first thing to understand about skiing is that the motive power is gravity and every thing you do, while you are skiing, is to control the effect of gravity. Many years ago I happen to be watching some children playing in the snow on the East cliff at Folkestone. They had a piece of tarpaulin which they spread out on the snow at the top of the hill, then they all climbed aboard, picking up the edge of the tarpaulin to hold onto and off they'd go, sliding down the hill due to gravity. What fun! But also due to gravity the whole shebang would rotate until the heaviest section, which was normally at the top when they started, *(probably because the clever children made sure they where not at the bottom to avoid other children falling on top of them,)* would finished up at the bottom, which would also unbalance some of the children and some would also fall off along the way, unbalancing everything again, causing the tarpaulin to rotate further until eventually they would all fall off. At which point they would return to the top of the hill with the tarpaulin to start all over again. Well the same sort of forces are also at work on skiers, which means it is necessary to learn techniques to be able to distribute your weight correctly to control your skis and keep your balance, to be able to go in a required direction, as you slide down the hill.

Personally, I think starting at the beginning is very important, you would be amazed at the number of beginners who think they don't need to bother with learning how to snow-plough and can sail off immediately doing parallel turns. To be honest it is not so difficult to start by doing parallel turns on the nursery slopes but I believe their problems will come when they get on the more difficult slopes without learning the basics of skiing properly. Therefore my advice to all beginners, if only for the sake of safety, is to start at the beginning with the snow-plough and work through each stage so that you will finish up being an all round competent skier. Anyway, there is nothing wrong with using the snow-plough as there are times when even expert skiers will use it, such as when they find themselves restricted by a crowd of other skiers in a small space on a sloping area.

Now the basic object of skiing down a snow covered hill is to be able to turn to your left or right when and where ever you wish to, and to be able to stop, and the ultimate dream is to be in control at all times and not fall down, surely that's not too much to ask for? After all, almost all holiday skiers manage to achieve a sufficient standard of skiing to enjoy themselves, but if you don't know how to, why bother? Well, because it's a lot of fun. I enjoyed learning to ski or trying to, from the very first day, every bit as much as I enjoy my skiing now, if you don't find it is fun, then it's probably not for you anyway. You either like skiing or you don't, it seems to me it's one of those black or white things, I don't think as far as skiing is concerned, there are any grey areas in between, although obviously some people will be keener and or better than others.

Having arrived at your resort and got yourself togged-out and fully equipped for the first time, you then need to deliver yourself at the ski school or on the nursery slopes. The nursery slopes are not for toddlers as you might think the name implies, the small toddlers from the nursery will be playing in the kindergarten, OK. So now that's all clear. The nursery slopes are in fact, an area that's meant for the use of all people learning how to ski, and normally it is "not" exclusively for beginners, so don't be surprised if a good skier comes swishing by. A nursery slope, which to beginners when they first see it may think it looks a bit like the Cresta run, will be an area with gentle gradients so that beginners can have the best chance of keeping control of their skis while they are learning, there will probably be one or two steeper bits to practise on as your skiing improves and as you gain more confidence. Don't worry if you find there are good skiers around, normal etiquette requires good skiers at all times to anticipate poor skiers and to be especially aware when skiing on nursery slopes to give poorer skiers a wide berth, so as to avoid the risk of having an accident.

On the point of etiquette on the pistes the basic principle is that anyone overtaking another skier is in general, responsible not to inconvenience the other skier, this does not relieve any skier of their responsibility to be aware of other skiers around them and also to avoid doing anything that might inconvenience other skiers, such as making a turn just in front of them, this includes having a good look around before starting to ski. As a last resort if you anticipate you are about to collide, try to turn away from danger. Ideally you should also be able to stop within your range of visibility or before reaching any point of danger, of course this assumes that you are always fully in control of your skis. Few people will be restraining their skiing to this level of caution because they generally have a higher opinion of their abilities than they deserve and anyway, a certain amount of risk is all part of the enjoyment of skiing. That should do for a start to keep you out of trouble, you will be able to pick up more points on skiing etiquette around the bars where there shouldn't be any shortage of people willing to advise you, regardless of whether they know anything about skiing etiquette or not.

If you have an accident or come across someone else who has had an accident, or for any other reason you think that it is necessary to warn any approaching skier that there is danger ahead, the universal signal is to stand up two crossed skis in the snow. Therefore, if you see two skis crossed standing up in the snow ahead of you, you will know there is danger ahead and to take care.

To start with, you will probably have joined the ski school and will have been allotted a beginners class, on the other hand, maybe you have elected to let a friend teach you or they may have even volunteered, or by whatever other arrangements you may have made to learn how to ski, it is now time to get started.

So let's look at what is happening when skiing. Essentially you ride on your skis, which are shaped so as to slide easily over the snow, and due to gravity you will travel down hill at a speed depending mainly on your weight, and the steepness of the hill. To control your speed and direction, it is necessary to understand how and why you need to move the distribution of your weight around on your skis, forwards, backwards, to the left and right to stay in control. You do not necessarily have to move your body significantly so much as just adjust the distribution of your weight from one foot to the other, or between the ball of your foot and your heel, or a combination of booth. The key to being in control of your skis is all about knowing where your weight should be, how to transmit the pressure produced by your weight onto your skis and the effect that it is having, in other words, you need to understand the dynamics of how your skis work. To ski you will need to keep your skis parallel to each other, or in a V shape with the point in front of you, because putting them in any other arrangement will cause you to fall down and I guess that will not please you too much.

4 FUNDAMENTAL SKIING PRINCIPLES

First we have to start with some definitions

The Piste.

Piste is French for a racing track, however as far as skiing is concerned it simply means a prepared track, and other areas prepared for skiing. Off piste obviously means leaving the prepared track.

The fall line & other expressions.

Next we need to define what the fall-line is, as it's name implies, it is "the line a ball will roll down the hill". It is important to know what the fall-line is because we will be referring to it all the way through the book, in fact it is just a more accurate way of saying downhill, for example when we refer to facing downhill or the fall line or leaning down the fall line, they all mean much the same thing. I only mention it because as far as I know, the expression "fall-line" is exclusive to skiing.

I will also be using other common expressions with obvious meanings like "up hill" or "upper" and "downhill" or "lower" to identify which ski, leg, shoulder or whatever part of your body I am referring to.

Edging your skis.

If you need to ski across the direction of the fall line then you will need to turn your skis onto their uphill edges, which is known as "edging your skis" or just "edging", to grip the snow which will allow you to go in an alternative direction other than straight down the hill.

The principles of how to ski

Now we have to consider some general rules, or principles that you will need to apply all the time you are skiing, before we start explaining how to make turns and actually ski. Ultimately everyone will develop their own version and style due to their individual bodies and consequently virtually everyone's techniques will vary slightly, however to be successful they will all need to be based on these principles. The basic principles that are explained in this book are really quite simple to understand, it's putting them into practise that's the problem. So first of all I will tell you what they are, and then explain why as well as how they work in practise, as we go along

To start with, always keep your body relaxed and free from any unnecessary tension, but this certainly doesn't mean allowing yourself to become at all droopy or floppy, just keep yourself as relaxed as you are when standing around at home, although ready and able to move or exert pressure anywhere and at any time as required.

"All the time you are skiing", you will always need to keep your knees bent, the reason for this will be explained later, but it's just that it's so important I thought I would plant that fact in your head right at the beginning.

Weight distribution.

When you are skiing down pistes, other than one rather obscure occasion which will be mentioned later, you must always be leaning forwards in a direction varying between the direction that you intend to go and the fall line, from now on, when I refer to this I will use the expression "leaning towards the fall line. (*However, when you reached the stage that you can start skiing off piste, then this does not necessarily always apply*).

You will be adjusting the distribution of your weight, depending on what you want to do, all the time. However, you will normally have most, or all of your weight on your lower ski, except when for some reason, which will be explained as we go along, to help you to make a particular manoeuvre, you "deliberately" transferred some, or all of your weight onto your uphill ski.

If you have too much of your weight on the balls of your feet it will have the effect of restraining, or braking your progress and therefore for beginners who may be fighting to stay in control, it's the natural thing to do. You must stop it at once. It will either cause you to come to a stop, or it will give you the opportunity to hesitate and lose confidence, and that won't help you to learn at all. Whereas, if you have more of your weight on your heels it will give you more control and have the effect of helping to propel you forwards, which of course is what you really want to do. You can try this in your home by standing up and pushing down on the balls of your feet, it is the same as if you have been running, when you need to put more of your weight on the balls of your feet to stop. Now try pressing down with more of your weight on your heels instead, while leaning forward with your knees bent and then you should have the feeling that you are being propelled or launched forward.

As a general rule, always keep your skis edged onto their "uphill edge", particularly your lower or downhill ski on which you will normally have most or all of your weight, by pointing your knees uphill or towards the mountain and also tucking your backside slightly in towards the mountain by moving your hips sideways, (*rather than by rotating them*). At the same time keep your shoulders relaxed so that it is easy for you face towards the fall line which will bring your uphill shoulder ahead of your downhill shoulder. Or if you are heading straight down the fall line, then you will need to keep your weight distributed equally on the "inside edge" of both of your skis by keeping your knees close together, and with your body leaning forwards and your shoulders relaxed.

The first skiing skill you will need to learn is how to move your weight around and between your skis to keep your balance and not fall down. As your weight is transferred onto your skis through your ski boots, for the practical purposes of learning how to ski, you can consider that your weight is transferred onto your skis at three separate points, first of all through your "heel", and then by pressing your shin gently against the "tongue of your ski boot", and finally through the "ball of your foot".

Now to explain it in more detail the following will apply for the purposes of transferring or distributing your weight, or to lower your weight, or to apply pressure, or push down on your skis, or however it may be described. First, to lower your body weight down, you will normally need at least half of your weight on your heel or heels, generally using the inside part of your heel, which is the main way you have to control the direction of your skis, as by pushing the heel of your skis sideways, you can change the direction or alter the course that you want to steer them. In other words you can say you also use your heels to steer your skis.

Then you need to press your shin against the tongue of your ski boot just enough so as to be aware that you are leaning forward. Especially while you are learning you will need to be aware "all the time that you are skiing" that you are pressing your shin gently against the tongue of the ski boot, as this is the easiest way to confirm that you are leaning forwards, because with a few rare exceptions, you need to be leaning forwards all the time you are skiing. It is very important that you remember that you can't press your shins against the tongue of your ski boots without leaning forwards. Pushing, or if you like, leaning against the tongue of your ski boot and pressing down on your heel, should help you to get the feeling that you are steering your skis as your weight pushes them forwards, down the piste.

This may make your shins sore, in which case you may need to get some pressure padding from the chemist to protect your shins. As I am getting older, I now find I have to use padding to protect my shins all the time while skiing.

Finally so as to be able to keep your balance, the rest of your weight will be pressing down through the ball of your foot, which you will do naturally without having to think about it. In fact when you start skiing, I suspect you will have to give a lot more thought to transferring your weight from the ball of your foot back onto your heel, (*so as to overcome your natural instinct when going down a hill when you are not skiing, to put more of your weight on the ball of your foot*).

When gently schussing straight down the fall-line on a "gentle slope" you will want your weight to be distributed between the balls of your feet and your heels, with just slightly more on your heels, and with just a detectable portion used to press your shin against the tongue of your ski-boot, so as to confirm you are leaning forward. From this position, you can then adjust the distribution of your weight, by shifting more of your weight back onto your heels, when the gradient of the slope gets steeper.

The correct direction for your hips.

I will be making many references to common skiing expressions, such as facing down the fall-line or down-hill, turn your shoulders to face down the fall-line or keep your body facing down the fall-line. The object of all these expressions is to help to ensure that your "hips" are turned the required amount towards the fall-line, which depends mainly on the difference between the heights of your skis, due to the steepness of the slope and the direction you wish to head relative to the fall line.

The position of your hips in your stance is very important, as it is through your hips that you apportion and distribute your weight correctly through your legs to your feet, and then onto your skis. It is almost certain that when your hips are facing in the right direction then your body will be turned towards the fall-line.

Your hips are the link between your body and your legs, and therefore are the most important part of your body while skiing. If your hips are not facing in the right direction but are turned towards the mountain, or uphill, then it will be very difficult if not impossible to distribute your weight correctly. Even by using brute force it will be very difficult, and it is more than likely that you will either lose control, or fall. As far as skiing is concerned, the rest of your body above your hips is really no more than ballast, although what you do with your ballast is very important, because it is essential to keep the centre of gravity of your ballast in the right place.

In practise it is not so easy to assess whether your hips are facing in the correct direction while you are skiing, however, it is easy enough to know which of your buttocks is higher than the other or if they are level, and as your buttocks are related to the position of your hips so that if your downhill buttock is lower than your other buttock, then your hips will automatically be facing towards the fall line. Therefore I think that it works out that the easiest way to keep your hips facing in the right direction is to concentrate on the position of your buttocks by normally keeping your downhill buttock lower than your uphill buttock. So if you do that then the problem of knowing that your hips are facing in the right direction is solved. However, in practice this is not so easy to do as your natural instinct normally is to try to keep your buttocks on the level by altering how much your knees are bent, so, as you are learning it will require some concentration by you.

When you are about to start off skiing and you want to turn to face down the fall-line, you can start by checking that your buttocks are in the correct position, actually finding the required direction to face is not very difficult as your hips will automatically feel more comfortable when they are in the correct position. Don't force your hips or anything else for that matter, to turn beyond the relaxed and comfortable position. (*In fact as a general rule when you are skiing, you must never force any of your limbs into positions that are uncomfortable*).

When making a manoeuvre or changing your stance, which requires you to alter the angle of your buttocks relative to the slope of the piste, I shall advise you to lower whichever of your buttocks is required and I suggest that you think in the same way, because it is likely that if I were to suggest that you raise your other buttock, you will automatically straighten your body and stop leaning forward, which will certainly not be what you want you to do. However, if I do want you to raise your body weight, then I might suggest you raise your buttocks, or one of them. If you just think of lowering which ever buttock is required, then you can rely on your other buttock to naturally assuming it's correct position.

Bend your knees

Everyone in the country knows that when you are skiing you need to bend your knees, if you like you can say that it is the first principal of skiing. "Bend zee neez" is also the expression regularly used by comedians when they want to introduce a skiing joke, probably because that is all they or any other non-skier knows about skiing. Well! As you control your skiing by the way you transfer your weight onto your skis and to do that you will need to be able to lean forwards and press your shins up against the tongue of your boot and at the same time, keep your heels with at least half of your weight firmly down in your boots,. It is "a fact of mechanics", that you can only do this if you "bend your knees". Therefore it is a cardinal rule of skiing that you must "always" keep your knees bent.

What I mean by the expression "a fact of mechanics" is that as in a machine, when a rod moves or a spindle rotates in a machine, any pieces connected to it in a correct arrangement, will move in a predictable manner. So the same applies in skiing, to achieve your aims or be able to ski, you must also have the limbs of your body in the correct arrangement or position, to be able to move in a predictable manner. I'm afraid it's the best analogy I can think of so I hope you are able to understand what I mean.

If your toes start to hurt while you are skiing it is probably because you have too much of your weight on the ball of your foot in your attempt to lean forward but without bending your knees enough. So if your toes start to hurt you will need to concentrate on bending your knees to apply more of your weight through your heels and if you do, you should also find that you also have a better control of your skis. The corollary does not necessary apply that if your toes don't hurt you can automatically assume that you haven't got too much weight on the ball of your foot. It is virtually impossible to put too much of your weight on your heels without immediately becoming aware thatyou have overdone it by the effect it has on your skiing, the chances are far more likely that you will not have enough of your weight on your heels.

26

Knees bent so that your thighs are nearly parallel with the ground.

(As a matter of interest in any sport, you tend to need to bend your knees before you make a forward move, your knees are the only joints in your body that bend backwards, therefore, apart from any other reason, they are the ones you use whenever you want to propel yourself forwards or upwards).

In general, while you are learning to ski you need to concentrate on remembering that you control your skis through your heels. Using your weight pressing down through the heel of your ski-boot to operate your skis, so that you can keep your skis parallel or slide your heels sideways into a turn, or to push the heel of your skis apart to make a V, and also when you want to edge your skis. If you don't bend your knees, then either you will not be leaning forward or your heel will rise in your boot or at least you will lift the weight off your heel which will stop you from being able to control your skis properly. If you like you can try it now without using any skiing equipment, stand up and lean forwards without bending your knees and you will find that you are unable to avoid your weight coming off your heels and transferring onto the ball of your foot, now bend your knees and as well as being able to lean forwards, you will find that now you can also return your weight onto your heels again.

As you use your heels to change the direction of your skis, to avoid using brute force you will want your skis to rotate round the pivotal point (*explained later*), which will normally be somewhere ahead of your ski-boots. Therefore it means you will normally have to slide the heels of your skis sideways to change the direction they are pointing or heading. It is difficult although not impossible on gentle slopes anyway, to steer your skis by using brute force to exert pressure through the ball of your foot without enough weight on your heels, but when the slopes get steeper, then it will become more strenuous and difficult, so it is better to start as you intend to carry on and bend your knees, so that you can press down through your heels to make a turn, and also press your shin against the tongue of your boot, to be sure you are leaning forwards.

Just because you are bending your knees, it is no guarantee that you are leaning forward, it is quite possible to bend your knees and sit back which won't help you to ski at all which is why you need to feel your shin pressing against the tongue of your ski boot all the time, to be sure that you are leaning forwards and not sitting back. There is one thing you can be sure of as a beginner, that unless you are double jointed, you will never bend your knees "too much", you may think you are, you may even think that you are bending your knees so much that your upper leg or thighs are parallel to the ground, even if they are, that would not necessarily be too much. Try it in front of a mirror, only if your knees are higher than your backside will you be bending your knees too much for a skiing beginner, so you can take it from me that, as a beginner you will never be bending your knees too much. You may see youngsters sitting on the heels of their skis as they schuss down the piste but they are only "putting on the style" and it is best if you forget about trying to emulate them until you are a fully competent skier, and only then if you are still young and agile enough.

Whenever you are bending your knees you will also need to bend at your hips and at your ankles, fortunately this is the natural thing for you to do so there is no need to give it any more thought, if you like, try that too it in front of a mirror too.

Your "centre of gravity" relative to the "central point of your weight"

Your "Centre of gravity", or the point at which your body is balanced if it is suspended, will be at the middle of your body, which for the average person is roughly half way between their navel and their spine, or possibly an inch or two higher or if you prefer in the area of your solar plexus, but somewhere in that region. Anyway the centre of gravity not only varies from person to person according to their shape, but it will move around with the movement of your body, or any part of it, which means that you will be slightly altering the position of your centre of gravity all the time.

By the "central point of your weight" I mean the point on the sole of your ski boot at which the distribution of your weight balances or the point at which you will balance if everything else supporting your weight at the sole of your ski boot is removed. While you are standing still on a level piste, normally you can expect the central point of where your weight is transferred through your ski boot onto your skis to be about halfway between your heel and the ball of your foot or the middle of your instep if you prefer. Even if you start to move it will still stay in the same place, what ever your speed is, as long as you retain the same stance and balance, but if you change either your stance or your balance so that for instance you do something so as to transfer more of your weight through your heels, then it will alter the position of the central point of your weight, in this case closer to your heel.

Make a careful note of the importance of the following:

The "effect" of the distribution of your weight will be decided by the position of your "Centre of gravity" relative to the position of the "Central point of your weight".

The "Central point of your weight" can move if you are pressing down through your heel then it will be at the heel through which you are pressing down or your weight is being transferred, and if you have no weight on your heels then it will most likely be at the ball of your foot. Normally it will be somewhere between the two, pro-rata to the amount of your weight that is distributed between your heel and the ball of your foot. If your weight

29

is being transferred to your skis through both of your boots, although not necessary evenly, then the "Central point of your weight" will be somewhere between your ski boots, pro-rata to the amount of weight on each boot. You may think I am being unnecessarily pedantic or meticulous, but I can assure you the truth is that a very small change in the relative positions of either your "Centre of gravity" or the position of the "Central point of your weight" will make a very significant difference to your balance and in turn will effect your ability to control of your skiing. In fact the relative position of your "Centre of gravity" and the "Central point of your weight" in theory is probably the most important feature you need to get right to be able to ski, although it is not enough on it's own.

Leaning forwards

The next basic principle we have to deal with is why you have to lean forwards when you are skiing, I shall be concentrating a lot on you leaning forwards or turning towards the fall-line, to overcome your natural instinct not to lean forwards. It is probably easier in fact to understand what would happen if you didn't lean forward.

When you are taking a walk down a hill, your natural instinct is to lean backwards so as to remain upright to keep your balance, because you expect your feet to grip the ground. This is the exact opposite of what you expect to happen when you are on skis on the snow, because you expect and even want them to slide forwards downhill, therefore when you are skiing, in simple terms, you need to do the opposite to what you do out walking. So, to keep your balance as you get carried along on your skis as they slide downhill, you will need to lean forwards.

Now to explain it in more detail: To keep your balance, so as to be able to control your skis while you are skiing, is all about the relative position between your Centre of Gravity and the Central point of your weight. If your Centre of Gravity is behind the Central point of your weight, then you will be leaning backwards and of course your skis will slide from underneath you downhill or ahead of you, and you will tip over backwards and fall down. If your Centre of Gravity is directly above the Central point of your weight then there will be no tendency to lean or fall in any direction, but your skis will still be able to slide downhill and if they do then the most likely result is again to cause you to tip over backwards.

So to stop you from tipping over backwards, you must lean forwards to create a force in the opposite direction. Or to put it another way, you will need to have your Centre of Gravity ahead or in front of the Central point of your weight, so that it will produce a force that will try to tip you forwards, head over heels. However your skis will still slide forwards which will remove, or counteract against the force trying to tip you head over heels, and will result in you riding downhill on your skis and that of course is the result that you will normally want. Incidentally, you also have a large portion of your skis ahead of your boots to lean against, which will also stop you from toppling forwards, head over heels.

Now to explain it technically, let's assume your weight is on your heels, by leaning forward far enough so that your Centre of Gravity is "ahead" of your heels, you will produce a lever "measured horizontally" from your heel, to the line of the vertical force produced by your weight, through your Centre of Gravity. The length of the lever multiplied by your weight will give a force that wants to tip you forwards not backwards, helping you to be able to keep control of your skis as you slide downhill. If you don't have any weight on your heels, but have all your weight on the balls of your foot, then the length of the lever will be reduced to the horizontal distance between the ball of your foot and your Centre of Gravity, this will reduce or worse still, may even remove the force stopping you from tipping over backwards and can cause you to fall, or lose control. It would therefore be fair to say that by keeping weight on your heels also gives you more stability as well as allowing you to control your skis. If you fall and you are leaning forwards pushing your weight down through your heels and are facing towards the fall-line, it will be for some other reason, like catching an outside edge et cetera, to be explained later.

So you see if you lean forwards you can't fall down backwards and you will not fall forwards either because of the long length of ski ahead of you to lean against as well as assuming that you will be moving forwards, which will counteract against any force trying to tip you head over heels, as the force of gravity propels you downhill, and so you will be skiing. Sorry, the short length of ski behind your ski boot will not stop you from falling backwards because it will follow the rest of your ski as it slides forwards down the hill. As has already been explained, if you bend your knees you can transfer your weight through your heels to control your skis and lean forwards at the same time. If you don't lean forwards but lean backwards, because of the arrangements of your body joints, you will start to sit down which will shift your Centre of Gravity backwards and that will cause you to tip over.

There is one sure way to confirm that you are leaning forwards and that is to be able to feel your shins pressing against the tongue of your ski boots, because you can only do that if you are leaning forwards.

Don't have your ankles clamped so tight in your ski boots so that you can't tell if they are pressing against the tongue of your ski boot or not. You should be able to slide a finger down between your boot and your ankle.

Putting it in a nutshell, I hope by now you will have realised that there is very little to stop you from falling backwards, therefore to avoid falling backwards, you must always lean forwards

Why your weight needs to be on your lower ski?

To give you stability and avoid falling, it is necessary to keep your weight on your lower ski, or at least the major portion of it depending on what you are doing at the time.

To help to explain this, lets take as an example a wheel that is suspended on it's axle so that it can turn freely, and then a weight is attached to the rim of the wheel to represent the weight of your body, the force of gravity will rotate the wheel until the weight representing the weight of your body is at the bottom. Well when you are skiing, if your weight is not already on your lower ski, much the same principle applies to your body weight.

If you accidentally put your weight on your upper ski, it will institute a force that will want to rotate you, so as to bring the ski with your weight on down to the bottom. Therefore, if "by mistake" you allow your weight to be on your upper ski, it will throw you off balance and that will probably cause you to fall, or lose control.

Transferring your weight to make a turn.

On the other hand if you want to make a turn, then by intentionally transfer your weight or some of it onto your upper ski, depending on how much and how quickly you want to turn, as just explained above, due to gravity your weight on your upper ski will want to move your upper ski to the bottom or below your other ski. If we go back to our analogy of the wheel but it is now tipped over to an angle nearly parallel to the slope, by putting a weight representing your body on the top or higher part of it's rim, representing the same as you putting your weight on your uphill ski, it will want to rotate due to the force of gravity, until the weight is at the bottom. In the same way as the wheel, when you transfer your weight onto your upper ski, and with the correct technique, due to gravity it will enable you to rotate or turn, towards the fall line, and then with the addition of your momentum to continue the turn until you are heading in the opposite direction, finishing up with the ski with your weight on at the bottom of our imaginary wheel, and below your other ski, which means you will have made a turn. At the same time your un-weighted ski should just follow round, trailing alongside the ski with your weight on. Yes, you may have to think about that for a bit, but I can assure you that transferring your weight onto your uphill ski will help you to make a turn, but only provided that you also use the correct technique.

That's the principle (*the techniques for making turns will come later*), you will also need to alter your stance to make a turn so that you don't lose your balance. I should point out that the steeper the gradient of the slope of the piste, the faster gravity will turn the wheel and therefore, you will also make a quicker skiing turn, alternatively, the more weight you transfer onto your upper ski will also help you to make a quicker turn.

I hope that by using the example a free turning wheel as a logical analogy, it has helped you to understand my theory. Strictly speaking I imagine that there are possibly plenty of reasons to argue about my diagnosis of the analogy of a weight being applied to the rim of a wheel, but that would be missing the point as I am simply trying to give you a visual picture, so as to help you to understand my explanation of what happens if you put some, or all of your weight, onto your uphill ski either intentionally or by accident. I just hope the way I have explained it, it will help you in practise. Of course while you are skiing, normally you will be adjusting the distribution of your weight between your skis all the time, to guide you on your way.

The General (or Default) Stance.

I have contrived a default stance which I shall call a "General stance" which you can use at anytime as a reference, whether you are stopped or while you are actually skiing or about to start skiing. The idea is that you can take this stance, which is made up of all the basic requirements that we have already mentioned to ski competently, when you are about to start off skiing, then all you will have to do is to adjust your general stance as you proceed to make different manoeuvres, which I will explain to you as we go along. How much simpler could it be? You can also use the general stance as a reference to check yourself against while you are actually skiing, so as to see if you are doing anything wrong at any time you feel you are having difficulties, or you are off balance and are trying to regain control of your skiing.

When adopting a general stance, the first and most important thing you need to do is to keep your body relaxed, much like you are when just standing around, remembering that any tension in your muscles will introduce additional unwanted equal and opposite forces into your skiing, so you need to avoid any tension, such as when you curl up your toes or clench your buttocks with anxiety when facing some difficulty like black ice for instance, which are a couple of the more common faults that can go unnoticed. Always keep your shoulders relaxed and facing towards the fall-line, or to put it another way, don't assume a stiff military like stance when skiing, as it will introduce unwanted tension, especially around your shoulders, which will make it difficult to lean forwards properly.

Now to assume the "general stance" on fairly level ground, lean forward so you can feel your shins pressing against the tongue of your ski boots to make sure that your Centre of Gravity is ahead of the Central point of your weight. (*After a little experience, when not on level ground you will be able to use your ski poles to stop you from moving downhill.*) Next, to be able to control of your skis you will need to bend your knees so that you can keep your heels placed firmly in the heel of your ski-boot, while at the same time have your shin pressing gently against the tongue of your ski-boot, to confirm that you are leaning forwards. To do this you also need to bend your ankles and at your hips. Alternatively, to make it more simple, you may like to think of it as assuming the normal position adopted when you are in the process of sitting down, but now leaning forwards with your shins pressing against the tongue of your ski boot, (*and without a chair*). Next you must lower your downhill buttock, and with your uphill ski ahead of your downhill ski so as to rotate your hips and body to face towards the fall-line, so that you can distribute more of your weight onto your lower ski. However, if you are skiing straight down the fall line then you will want your weight to be evenly distributed between your skis, then your buttocks should be level.

You need to allow your arms to hang down relaxed and more or less vertically at your sides, which as you are leaning forwards will mean that your hands will be slightly ahead of your body, any lifting of your forearms while you start learning is likely to introduce some unwanted stress across your shoulders. Later on you will want to move your arms to use your ski poles, but normally this will be part of a skiing manoeuvre and will probably be done by swinging your arm into a new position, such as to plant your ski pole in the snow. OK. When you have become a sufficiently competent, then you will be able to open and bend your arms and hold your ski poles more horizontally and pointing backwards, to assist you in keeping your balance and to check that your shoulders are facing towards the fall line, as well as adding a little style to your skiing, but really that is not included as part of the general stance.

While you are putting all your body bits and pieces in their correct positions, make sure you keep yourself feeling comfortable and relaxed, particularly across your shoulders to avoid introducing any unwanted strains and stresses or pressures. Just in case you should think of trying, it doesn't "ever" help to artificially tilt or force your shoulders or for that matter any other part of your body, up or down or any other abnormal posture at any time when skiing.

To summarise: To assume the general stance, relax but don't droop, lean forwards with your knees bent so that you can have more weight on your heels while being able to feel your shin pressing slightly against the tongue of your boot, also bending at your ankles and hips. Lower your downhill buttock to transfer your weight onto your downhill ski, with your uphill ski slightly ahead. Keeping your arms relaxed at your sides holding your ski poles pointing slightly backwards and with your body facing towards the fall line.

To regain control.

When you are skiing and especially for a beginner, if you feel you are losing control, in which case you will almost certainly have stopped leaning forwards, as a general rule in an emergency to regain control and to avoid falling, you will need to bend your knees more to lower your centre of gravity or your body weight, and by pushing down on your heels at the same time to throw or launch your body forwards, swinging your arms forwards which will move your centre of gravity forward, as well as adding momentum, (*much the same as a skier when making a ski jump, after whizzing down the ramp to gather speed and then launches into the air to make a jump forwards as far as he can; or a swimmer launches into a dive at the start of a race,*) also by pushing down through your heels you will improve your stability and help you to increase the control of your skis. To get the feel of what you need to do in an emergency, practice doing it while you are in control of your skiing, until you are satisfied you have got the hang of it. If for nothing else after doing that you should still fall, at least the more you have bent your knees the lower your body will be, so the less distance you will have to fall, so that you are less likely to hurt yourself, how much more comforting can it be for you knowing that?

If you feel you are losing control of your skiing and yet you feel sure that you are leaning well forward, then it is almost certain that too much of your weight is on the balls of your feet, which means you need to bend your knees more to be able to transfer more of your weight onto your heels to regain control of your skiing.

Falling and getting up.

If you allow your skis to cross each other then you are almost guaranteed to fall because the ski on top will be held off the snow by the ski underneath it, and you will not be able to do anything with the ski which is underneath because it is trapped by the ski on top of it, so hey presto! Down you go. Therefore, it is very important never to let your skis cross.

After falling, your next problem is how to get up? Even if your skis are crossed, and or, are stuck or trapped in anyway in the snow, first of all you must somehow struggle to manoeuvre your body to be above your skis so that your skis are downhill, to achieve this, you wouldn't be the first person to roll themselves head over heels. Believe me, it is impossible to get up if your skis are not below your body, unless of course you have someone to help you, even then it will still be easier if you first get your skis below you. If your skis are crossed then it will be necessary to first of all uncross them, before you can do anything else to try to get up. Only as a last resort, if they are firmly held in the snow, it may very well be necessary to release your bindings to free your boot from your ski.

Once you have your skis below you, you will now need to arrange them so that they are at right angles to the fall line and then draw them up as close to you as you can and so that they are on their edges. Next you will need to push your body up over your skis, to do this, you may need to grip your ski poles together and place them in the snow about a foot or two above you, in a position that is convenient for you to push yourself up and over your skis, until you are in a position to raise your body so as to be able to stand up. When the piste is nearly flat is when it will require the maximum amount of effort on your part to get up.

5 SNOW PLOUGHING AND THE KICK TURN

The snowplough and stopping.

At last we have reached the point at which we can actually start talking about moving on skis, or skiing.

For reasons of safety, you will almost certainly start by learning how to do the snowplough, because before you start schussing downhill on skis, it is better if you know how to stop, and for beginner, the easiest way to do that is by using the snowplough.

Technically the snowplough is the easiest exercise to do while at the same time staying in control and being able to keep your balance and not to fall, however, physically it is the most arduous and is therefore harder work. Once you are able to snowplough and to do snowplough turns and stop, you can then progress in stages to traversing, schussing and then to do the stem Christy turn, before eventually doing parallel turns, all of which become technically more difficult, although at the same time they are also progressively less strenuous to do.

The snowplough.

First of all to do a straight down the hill snowplough, choose a gentle slope so you won't go too fast. You can use your ski poles stuck in the snow, in the direction of the fall line away from you to lean on to stop you moving forwards, so that you can then turn towards the fall-line to get into position to assume the general stance. Keeping the front tips of your skis fairly close together, well about, give or take 3"- 4" (8-10 cm) apart, so the tips don't touch so as to avoid getting your skis crossed, press outwards with your heels, to push the rear end of your skis apart so as to form a V shape with your skis, hence the term snowplough, (*that is, the old horse drawn snowploughs of yesteryear before lorries and tractors arrived on the mountains, which were made up of two large planks of wood stood on their edges and joined into a V shape and pulled by horses to clear the snow off the roads*). Edge your skis on their inside edges by keeping your knees bent and close together and pressing down through the inside edge of your ski-boots. By edging your skis with your weight on their inside edge, facing down the fall-line and leaning forwards with your shins pressing against the tongue of your ski boots, and your weight evenly distributed between your skis, in this position your skis can grip the snow so you can stop yourself from moving forward on a quite steep slope. Now you can ease your weight off your ski-poles until you are happy that you are not going to move forwards and then take them out of the snow and hold them in the normal position at your sides with your shoulders relaxed.

Once you are in the snow plough position, reduce the amount of edging until you start to move down the hill but still keeping the back ends of your skis apart, once you have started moving you will be snowploughing. As you start moving make sure you don't allow the tips of your skis to cross over, which will certainly cause you to fall. If you want to stop again, keeping your knees close together, edge your skis more by increasing your weight on the inside edge of your ski-boots until you stop, after you have done this exercise a few times to get the feel of it, you will then want to turn, that is to make a snowplough turn.

Snowplough Turn.

After you have started snowploughing down the fall-line, to make a snowplough turn and let's say you want to turn to the left, you will need to transfer some of your weight onto your right ski by lowering your right buttock, (*this does not require any major change in your stance, it's much the same as when you transfer your weight from one foot to the other while you are walking or jogging*) you just need to feel a slight lowering your right buttock as you transfer your weight, this action will also help to tilt your hips in the right direction and reduce your weight on your left ski. Bend your left knee more, as you lean slightly to your left into the turn, much as you might lean naturally into a turn while you are jogging, or riding a bicycle, but don't bend at the waist. Once you have more weight on the inside edge of your right ski than your left, while continuing to lean forward with your shoulders all square and facing towards the fall line, you will start to turn to your left, (*remember the weight on the wheel*). When you want to stop turning, you will need to return some of your weight back onto your left ski, the reason for that is that if you were snowploughing straight down the fall-line when you started, after making a turn you must now be skiing across the fall-line. I suppose you could say that as you are now skiing across the fall line, that you are making a snow-plough "traverse" explained in the next chapter, but I have never heard anyone call it that. Anyway, as with traversing, to keep in control of your skiing and to maintain a steady course, you will now need to have more of your weight on your lower right ski, instead of having it evenly distributed between your two skis as you did when you skied straight down the fall line.

Since you started snowploughing down the fall-line, by turning to the left you will be heading across the fall-line which will be less steep, so that you will also slow down, or for that matter you may even come to a stop, if you turn too much.

The next exercise will normally mean making a turn in the opposite direction to your right. This will now require you to transfer more of your weight back onto your left, or uphill ski, by lowering your left buttock, which will automatically cause you to raise your right buttock, now lean slightly to your right while also bending your right knee more to help you to ease your weight off your right ski, in the same way as you did to make a turn to the left. A word of caution, before you start on this part of the exercise, you have turned to your left from skiing down the fall-line, so that when you start turning to your right, you will be returning towards the fall-line again, so all things being equal, the slope will be getting steeper which means you can expect to start going faster. However, as you keep making the turn to your right, once you have passed the direction of the fall-line and you continue

40

making your turn, the slope will start to become less steep again, and so you will start to slow down. If you want to stop yourself from going faster, you can always reduce your speed by edging your skis more.

A simple principle to remember when skiing is that when making a turn, you should always have more weight on your outside ski.

Relatively, snowploughing is quite hard work and hopefully as you progress it will not be the style of skiing you will be doing for long, but it is also the easiest way to keep in control of your skis and since you have just started skiing, for the time being we will stick to snowploughing.

To review our progress, we started off snowploughing down the fall line and then by shifting our weight from one ski to the other, by lowering our right buttock we are able to turn to the left, and then by lowering our left buttock, turn to the right. It's a start and will get you around the nursery slopes but it is too clumsy for anything steeper. Well! If you want to use it on steeper gradients you can, but only up to a point and as I've said it will be hard work.

I remember when I first started skiing, being in a ski school class coming all the way down the mountain from the top, on a green standard piste. In fact, it was really just a path used by walkers in the summer time. As all of us were only able to do a snowplough, when we were finished our legs were absolutely shattered, but since it was our first run from the top of the mountain we were also totally elated, I expect it's because we were more easily pleased in those days.

If after making a snowplough turn you change from doing a snowplough to traversing, explained in the next chapter, by simply allowing your skis to come together, that will make skiing very much easier, only opening your skis again into a V when you want to make your next snowplough turn. There are many people who are quite happy skiing around, day after day just making snow plough turns and traversing in between, of course you need plenty of room to make your turns and normally you can not traverse down narrow paths either, so you will have to resort to the snowplough. Admittedly it's not very ambitious, but who is to say what they should do as long as they are enjoying themselves and so long as they stay on relatively easy pistes.

Kick turn

You need to be stopped before you can do a kick turn. It is basically a safety manoeuvre to get out of trouble, such as if you meet some black ice or a bare patch on the piste and therefore want to turn round and go in another direction. The idea is to be able to turn round and face in the opposite direction, without needing to move.

First you must place your skis at 90°, or at right angles if you prefer, to the fall-line, facing down the fall-line place your ski poles in the snow either side of you, up hill and behind you. Then transfer your weight from your downhill ski onto your uphill ski and by leaning back also putting some of your weight onto your ski poles. Lift up your lower ski and place it's heel in the snow below and next to the point of your uphill ski, so that it is standing upright with it's pointed end in the air. Now lower the pointed end of your lower ski and at the same time rotate it 180° away from you so that it is pointing in the opposite direction to your upper ski. Now transfer your weight back onto your lower ski, which is the one that is now pointing in the new direction, lift your uphill ski and swing it 180° around the back of your other leg to place it below and alongside your other ski and then transfer your weight onto your new lower ski. I have just described to you the elegant way to do the kick turn, as taught to me by my ski teacher.

Some generally younger and more agile people, who's limbs and knee joints are more supple, find this an easy exercise to do but I'm not one of them. Although I was able to do my own version in my own style at one time, I doubt that I would be able to do it at all now as my rheumatic limbs and arthritic joints are far too stiff, just the thought of trying, starts them creaking and cracking. Fortunately it is a long time ago since I had to do it in anger to get out of trouble and hopefully I will never need to do it again.

Never-the-less try it, as long as you are young enough, under 50 anyway, and your joints are still supple enough it shouldn't cause you any difficulties, it is well worth knowing how to do it as you never know when it might come in useful. If you like you can consider it as being a new way to find out how supple your joints are, so there you are, how much more incentive could you want than that?

6 THE SCHUSS AND TRAVERSING

Schuss

The "schuss" is a pretty straight forward exercise, it simply means skiing more or less straight down the fall-line. To schuss, you just need to place your ski poles in the snow downhill of you to lean on, while facing down the fall line you assume the general stance, keeping your feet comfortably side by side, anything up to about a foot (30cm) apart is acceptable and by keeping your knees together with your weight on the inside edges of your skis to avoid catching an outside edge and falling. Once you are in position just let yourself go straight down the fall line and you will be schussing. Sometimes ski teachers want you to keep your feet close together which may look stylish, but when just doing a straight down the fall line schuss it is not essential, otherwise however, you should normally try and keep your skis close together so as to be able to keep a better control of your skiing, of course other than when snow ploughing or making a manoeuvre.

Simply schussing will give you no control over your speed, the steeper the gradient the faster you will go, and the faster you go the more you must bend your knees and lean forward. However, at least the more you bend your knees, the more you will reduce your height and lower your body, which means you will lower your centre of gravity and that will give you more stability, which is why racing skiers crouch down to improve their stability and keep control of their skis, as well as reducing their wind resistance.

Catching an outside edge.

Catching an outside edge as it is called, is a bit like tripping up on the edge of a paving stone. To avoid catching an outside edge on something like a piece of black ice or just some hard snow, a stone or anything else protruding above the snow, you need to edge your skis on their "inside" or "uphill" edge particularly your lower ski with your weight on. In fact you need to cultivate the habit of remembering to edge your lower ski, on which you will normally have your weight, onto it's uphill edge all the time you are skiing. Even when you are schussing you need to keep your knees close together to be sure that your weight is on the inside edge of your skis, otherwise you will be liable to catch an outside edge, causing you to trip up as you might say and fall.

To avoid looking foolish around the bars, it is not a good idea to say you tripped up while skiing, but if you say you caught an outside edge. Well! You will almost sound professional.

If instead of schussing straight down the fall-line, you want to proceed at an angle to the fall-line, then that is known as "traversing". When you are traversing, because instead of going straight down the fall-line you are going across it, you will have a downhill ski which will be lower than your other ski. You may think the difference between the level of your skis on a gentle slope is insignificant but I can assure you that even the very minutest difference will make a difference to you being able to distribute your weight onto your skis properly to keep control of your skis and your balance. If it helps, think how much a tall piece of furniture, like a hat stand, wobbles if the floor is not level to realise how easy it is to be thrown off balance.

The difference between the level of your skis will depend on two factors, the steepness of the hill or it's gradient and the angle between the fall-line and the direction you are traversing. When traversing it is necessary to alter your stance so as to put more or maybe all of your weight on your lower ski, depending on how steep the gradient of the hill is. To achieve the correct stance to be able to have more of your weight comfortably on your lower ski for traversing, it is a simply matter of mechanics that you will need to have your "upper ski ahead of your lower ski", and to be able to turn your lower ski onto it's uphill edge you need to tuck your lower knee in behind your upper knee, to help also keep your backside slightly tucked in side ways towards the mountain.

You might like to try a little experiment at this stage, stand up with your feet together, side by side, ensure you are relaxed, now rotate your hips let's say to your left as far as you can comfortably, which will be about 45°, now look down at your legs and you should find that your left leg is bent at the knee and your weight will be on your right leg, which is how you want to be when you are traversing to your left.

Traversing

You can therefore see it is natural to use the same stance when traversing, it just needs to be modified a bit so that your weight is on your lower ski, for example when traversing to your left, by lowering your downhill or right buttock. So that you can lean forward comfortably you will also require your uphill ski to be ahead of your lower one. Keep your knees bent and pointed slightly to your left or towards the mountain so that your weight is on the inside or uphill edge of your skis, with your hips and body facing towards the fall-line to help you to assume the proper traversing stance, with your shins gently pressing against the tongue of your ski boots, keeping your backside tucked in towards the mountain.

A large part of your skiing will be taken up with traversing, but the same applies whether on gentle slopes when the difference in height between your skis is very small or on steeper slopes when the difference will be greater. It therefore follows that the difference between the height of your skis will decide the direction that your hips should face, and how much your lower buttock is below your upper buttock, also, how far your upper ski is ahead of your lower ski and with your lower knee tucked in behind your upper knee, pointed towards the mountain so that your skis are edged with your weight on the inside edge of your lower ski to avoid catching an outside edge, it won't work satisfactorily any other way. To be comfortable, you will also need to have your shoulders facing towards the fall line, which means that your uphill shoulder will be ahead of your lower ski shoulder. Only when you have everything positioned correctly will you find a comfortable stance for traversing without any extraneous compression or tension strains on your muscles to make skiing hard work.

It will be as well to remember that as a general rule when you are skiing, when you have found the correct stance it will feel more comfortable, without any stress in your muscles and therefore it will be less strenuous and easier to ski.

When traversing with your lower ski edged with your weight on it's "uphill edge", it will stop your skis from sliding sideways down the fall-line as well as stopping you from catching an outside edge, so you can also use this edging of your skis to cut into, or grip, or to push against the snow by pushing down on the inside of your lower ski to help you to slow down, and control your speed.

Because modern ski boots come up above your ankles, by making sure your lower knee is pointing towards the mountain or uphill, it will help to ensure your lower ski is turned onto it's inside or uphill edge. With the old fashioned leather boots, which did not come so far up your ankles, you had to use your ankles to edge your skis and that probably explains why more ankles and shins got broken before the introduction of the modern plastic ski boots. So give a big hurrah for the modern plastic ski boot, even though you can't dance in them, well not elegantly anyway.

46

I hope by now you will have realised how all the different actions you are required to take to ski are interrelated with each other, which means that if you get just one wrong, you will upset the whole shebang which will stop you from skiing properly.

If you want to feel you are traversing correctly and also to be stylish at the same time, keep your skis close together with your lower knee tucked in behind your upper knee. It will not be so easy on the more difficult pistes with bumps known as moguls to keep your skis together and your lower knee tucked behind your upper one all the time, but it is still worth trying for, because as a general rule, the closer together your skis are, the less difference there will be between the height of your skis, which will make it easier to keep your balance. At the very least keep your knees together, because if you can, making turns or manoeuvres is much easier and maybe surprisingly your stance will feel more stable. To complete your stance for traversing, rotate your hips, body and shoulders so that you are leaning towards the fall-line.

"Moguls" are just heaps of snow in humps and or ridges formed by skiers making turns, and then the valleys between the moguls get scoured out, making the valleys deeper.

7 UNWEIGHTING SKIS TO TURN

Unweighting your ski

When skiers are discussing manoeuvres they will use the word "unweight" such as "to unweight your lower ski", which, as you might expect means to reduce or take the weight off your lower ski. So before we go any further I think it will be as well to explain how to unweight your ski or skis.

There are basically two ways to unweight both of your skis together. A sufficient effect can be achieved by either skiing uphill over a bump which will raise your body weight off your skis, or by simply physically raising your body by raising your buttocks to unweight your skis, either of which will unweight your skis sufficiently although only momentarily, for you to make a manoeuvre, (*or alternatively by jumping, when for a moment there will be no weight on your skis while you are in the air, however, jumping on skis is really for advanced skiers, probably when skiing down moguls or more advanced trick skiing and not very easy for adult learners, not that I particularly want to deter anyone from jumping, especially if they are young and agile if that's what they feel like doing.*)

In the course of making a turning manoeuvre, you will need to unweight your downhill ski on which you would normally have your weight, to transfer your weight onto your uphill ski, in which case you again have two alternatives. Either you can push down on your lower ski to "push" your body weight upwards or alternatively you can lower your body weight down onto your uphill ski to "lift" your body weight off your lower ski. The significance between the two methods is the effect it has on the position of your hips. If you push down on your lower ski your hips will tend to face uphill which will encourage you to turn uphill, and if you lower your body weight down onto your uphill ski to lift you weight off your lower ski, your hips will naturally turn downhill and that will encourage you to turn downhill. Therefore in general terms, if you want turn uphill, press down on your downhill ski and conversely, if you want to turn downhill, as you would in the normal course of skiing down a piste, then you will need to lower your body weight down onto your uphill ski, to transfer your body weight

Years ago, when I first started in ski-school we were taught the following routine when we were being instructed on how to transfer our weight onto the other ski, although it was not explained why, we were just told to go through this routine to transfer our weight. First we were told we must bend our lower ski knee more, to lower our body, then to raise our body to take our weight off our lower ski and finally to lower our weight back down onto our upper ski. For beginners trying to work through this sequence took forever and a day, to say nothing of feeling like a girl in the chorus line as we bobbed up and down. It was hardly surprising then that on skis that anyway were far too long, to say nothing of the fact that we were also told to lean out, instead of just keeping our weight on our outside ski when making a turn, that we invariably fell down. Come to think of it, we would probably have learnt more if we had been bobbing up and down in a chorus line, although not necessarily about how to ski, however I'm digressing.

In fact there is a very important reason why you should "not" follow this sort of routine, because after you have lowered your body by bending your lower knee and then to lift your weight up, you are almost certain to first push downwards on your lower ski so as to lift your weight up and that will increase the pressure on your lower ski, and the effect of that is to make you turn uphill, which is in the opposite direction to the turn you would normally want to make, therefore it will not help you at all. So the important lesson to be learnt from all this is that you mustn't press down on your lower ski when you want to transfer your body weight onto your upper ski.

Transferring your weight to make a turn.

When you are skiing and wish to make a turn quickly, basically, you need to transfer your weight quickly. Making quicker turns will give you more control of your skiing so as to be able to go wherever you want. The most effective and efficient way to control the distribution and transferring of your weight is by the raising and lowering your buttocks much as you do all the time when you are walking or probably more accurately when you are jogging, except that now you need to slightly exaggerate it.

To make a turn you have to raise your body to unweight your lower ski and then to transfer your weight onto your upper ski, all in one movement. Well! The simple trick to transferring your weight quickly, without pushing down on your lower ski, is to simply lowering your uphill buttock to lower your body weight straight down on your uphill ski, and that will automatically raise your downhill buttock and your body and your body weight, to un-weight your lower ski, all without pressing down on your lower ski, and so you will have transferred your weight onto your uphill ski, all in one movement.

Please make sure you have read, learned, and inwardly digested the bold section, as it is crucial to being able to competently make a quick turn. This action will also tilt your hips into the opposite direction ready to be in the correct line when you have completed your turn. Eureka! It's really no different to what you do while you are simply jogging along the road, when you are continuously raising your body between each step as alternately you move your buttocks up and down to transfer your weight from one foot to the other.

When you want to make a turn, if you don't transfer your weight onto your uphill ski first, then you can only make a turn by using brute force.

I don't know because I didn't start skiing until I was about 28, but I suspect that while children are still agile and flexible they are able to move their weight around effortlessly without thinking about it, probably up and until about roughly their mid teens. But if they start learning to ski after that then they will probably need to start thinking more about what they are doing to transfer their weight, and that will bring them more into the adult beginners school.

When you intend to make a turn, there is one thing you need to be careful of when pushing down on your upper ski to unweight your lower ski to transfer your weight, which is as a reaction to pushing down and outwards on the inner edge of your outside ski to make a turn, you make sure you don't push your backside out in the opposite direction, as this will dilute the force from leaning into the turn to push outwards on your ski. If you do allow your backside to move sideways it will also reduce your control or you may even lose control of the manoeuvre altogether, to say nothing of making it harder work. You therefore need to concentrate on keeping your backside steady and in line with the rest of your body, as you push outwards when making a turn.

Children seem to be able to do theses manoeuvres without knowing anything about the principles or theories which I suppose is because their bodies are more agile than adults.

8 STEM CHRISTY TURNS. SLIDE – SLIPPING. STOPPING

Stem Christy turns

To progress from making snowplough turns and traversing, having learned to unweight our skis, the next step is to learn how to make Stem Christy turns. You might say the Stem Christy turn is half way between a snowplough turn and a parallel turn and I therefore think it is well worth learning, although with the introduction of carving skis, I understand a lot of instructors skip Stem Christy turns and move straight on to doing parallel turns. But, as I don't want you to feel you have been deprived, I will explain how to do a Stem Christy turn and then you are free to choose whether to ignore them if you so wish, or not.

Let's start for example by traversing to your right, so as to make a Stem Christy turn to your left. First assume the general stance, but heading to traverse towards your right, so you will need to tuck your backside in towards the mountain to your right and lower your left buttock to rotate your hips to face down the fall-line, and move your right ski ahead of your left ski with your left knee behind your right knee, with your weight on your left ski and with your left shin pressing against the tongue of your ski boot to traverse to your right.

Starting off by traversing to your right, to make a turn to your left. First you have to slide your right ski heel out, but keep the tips of your skis close together and your hips facing down hill, to form as you might say, "half" the V you would have made to make a snowplough turn. Then transfer your weight onto the upper or right hand ski by lowering your right buttock, pressing down on the inside right heel, and against the tongue of your right ski boot to make sure you are leaning forwards, all at the same time, while leaning slightly to your left into the turn, but don't bend sideways at your waist. Keeping your weight on the outside ski, in this case your right hand ski, but on it's inside edge, by keeping your knees together with right knee pointing into the turn, again much the same as when you do a snowplough turn. To help you to avoid putting any weight on your left ski, it will be necessary to bend your inside, in this case your left knee a lot more. You will then find that as your weight comes onto your right ski you will turn to your left, while keeping your shoulders facing down the fall-line, and your right shin leaning against the tongue of your right boot.

When you have completed the turn, still keeping your weight on your right hand ski which will now have become your lower ski, bring your skis together again, with your upper ski ahead of your lower ski and still facing down the fall-line, but with your left shoulder ahead of you, and your right knee now tucked in behind your left knee and with your backside again tucked in towards the mountain to traverse to your left. In this way, you will have completed a Stem Christy turn. If you transfer your weight quickly you will turn quickly, which means that you will pass the fall line quickly so you will minimise the amount of time to gather any extra speed.

It will require a lot more practise than is needed to learn to do a snowplough turn. Sometimes instructors will advise you to place your ski pole in the snow to help you to unweight your lower ski and to launch yourself forwards to make the turn, but if you do, don't put any weight on it.

To use your ski-pole in the above example, when you are turning to your left, as you start to slide the tail of your right hand ski out, you can also swing your left ski pole forwards and place it close to the left of the tip of your left hand ski which will automatically help you to raise your left buttock to unweight your left ski and to transfer your weight onto your right ski. The placing of a ski pole in the snow roughly at the point slightly ahead of you, where you want to make your turn, to help you to unweight your lower ski, other than when making a snow plough turn, is a common skiing practise.

Once you have mastered the Stem Christy turn, you will be able to venture out onto steeper slopes than with the snowplough turn. All in all you will have much better control of your skiing and that means you can safely ski faster too.

Side slipping.

We are now at about the right stage to learn to side slip. "Side slipping" is a technique that can be used as a last resort to get down difficult sections of a piste and needs to be mastered before risking for instance, a difficult slope while doing Stem Christy turns.

Essentially it is the same as traversing without moving forward. So before you start "side slipping" assume the same stance as for traversing accept that you now need to have your skis at right angles to the fall-line so that you will remain stopped but still with your up-hill ski ahead of your lower ski,. From this position, lower your downhill buttock to put virtually all your weight on your lower ski, with your knees and backside pointing into the mountain to heavily edge your skis, rotating your hips and shoulders so that you can lean directly down the fall-line. Allowing up to half of your weight onto the ball of your foot, slowly reduce the amount of edging until you start to slide sideways down the fall-line and that is what is referred to as "side slipping". You can control the speed of your side slipping by adjusting the amount of edging, by how much your knees point towards the mountain. If you have reached the stage where you can competently do everything up to a Stem Christy turn, side slipping should be a piece of cake. Once you can side slip, it is easy enough to combine it with traversing by transferring more of your weight from the ball of your foot back onto your heel, so that you can move ahead while you are still side slipping. You will then be able weave your way down the piste, turning and slipping and sliding with the best of them.

Stopping

Since now you are in such good control of your skis, you will have automatically learnt to make small adjustments to the direction you are skiing by simply adjusting the proportion of your weight on each of your skis.

Ah yes! But when you are weaving your way down the piste with the best of them, how do you stop, other than changing into a snowplough? It's so obvious it seems hardly worth mentioning, you simply turn up-hill when you are bound to come to a stop, but make sure you are still leaning forward and facing downhill. Well that's the principle, but also make sure you don't overdo it because your pivot point (explained in the nest chapter) will return to your ski boots and if you are actually pointing uphill when your pivot point will be behind your ski boots then instead of just stopping, you may start to slide backwards and more than likely finish up falling. To turn up-hill quickly to come to a stop, you need to bend your knees and leaning forwards more, lowering your downhill buttock to push down on the heel of your downhill ski to make the turn, but in this case, once you have started turning, you can also help to brake your speed by pushing down more on the balls of your feet, and edging your skis as much as possible by pointing your knees into the turn to grip the snow, all in one movement, which will make your skis skid round in short order, or if you prefer, make a turn in a short distance. This is sometimes called a "swing stop", a far too dramatic expression for me to use so I shall use the more normal term of "stop turn". Oh yes! us old timers can be such a bore at times, never mind, just don't take any notice of us, then we can carry on explaining how to ski.

9 THE PIVOT POINT

Pivot or pivotal point definition

One of the first things you will soon realise when you start learning how to ski is that it is more difficult to make a turn, or to turn on your skis, when you are stopped or only moving very slowly, than it is when you are skiing at a more normal speed. The reason for this is the position of the skis' pivot point or pivotal point, (*or centre of turn or turning point or turning centre or whatever else you like to call it*) I shall refer to it as the pivot or pivotal point which moves relative to your speed, and also to the angle that your skis are pointing either uphill, downhill, or on the level.

If you can understand the principles of how the pivot point moves, then you will find it is a lot easier to understand how to ski over moguls, which is when I think understanding how the position of the pivot point moves will help you the most to understand it's effect on your skiing, because as you ski over moguls your skis will either be pointing up or down a lot more than when skiing down a normal piste. The position of the pivot point is also more significant when you start skiing at greater speeds, as you start making parallel turns.

(Also if you are unable to find anything else to talk about and you want to risk it, I think you will also find that it will be a handy help to stimulating a discussion over a beer in the evenings. However, should it be necessary, be prepared to duck quickly.)

If you are one of those people who are able to learn how to ski by just following the given instructions, without knowing 'why' , then it's probably not necessary for you to know anything about the pivot point or how it moves, and therefore you don't need to bother with it at all.

I think the pivot point can best be explained as the point around which your skis rotate when you are altering or changing the direction you wish to go. Alternatively, we may use the analogy of a wheel again to give us a kind of diagram to see where the pivot point is, (*whoever would have thought we needed so many wheels to explain how to ski?*)

Anyway, if we take one of the spokes of a "rotating wheel" lying on it's side to represent you on your skis as you slide the heel of your skis sideways to make a turn, then the centre, or hub of the wheel will represent the position of the "pivot point" around which your skis are sliding sideways.

Now to define the pivot point technically: Any "stationary" vessel floating in a fluid, or for that matter a "stationary" balloon floating in a gas, will have it's pivot point at it's centre of balance. If it then starts to move on the level, the pivotal point will move away from the centre of balance of the vessel or balloon, in the direction it is moving, and at a distance relative to the speed of the vessel or balloon. The pivot point of the vessel or balloon will move the maximum distance, relative to it's speed, when it is on the level or on an even keel. If the vessel or balloon is not on the level but trimmed upwards or downwards then the distance the pivot point moves relative to it's speed will be reduced, until the amount it is trimmed is enough to stop the pivot point from moving ahead at all, at which point if it is trimmed further, the pivot point will start moving backwards from vessel or balloon's centre of balance. That, I think, fairly defines the pivot point and how it moves.

Attention, Achtung, I'm in a hurry or please excuse me

The pivot point also applies to aeroplanes and gliders too, but technically because they can only stay aloft as long as they are moving, aeroplanes and gliders are not strictly speaking, floating in the air, but the pivot point doesn't know that and so behaves in the same way as though they are floating.

The effect of the pivot point.

The tricky bit is this, for the purposes of explaining how the pivot point effects your skis, you have to accept that as your skis are not fixed or held to the ground anywhere and can slide in any direction, and therefore they can also in effect be said to be floating on the snow. When you are standing still and on the level, the pivot point will be roughly at the middle of your skis boots and you will only be able to turn as a result of rotating your boots. For simplicity lets assume for the moment that we are on a fairly level piece of snow. If the skis move forwards the pivot point will also move forwards, ahead of your boots along your skis, and will reach the tips of your skis at about the speed you can run, lets say about 6 to 7 m.p.h. or roughly 10 k.p.m. so that it will create a "lever" between your heels and the pivot point. If you go faster then the pivot point will move further ahead beyond the tips of your skis. Or for that matter, if the skis move backwards, then the pivot point will move backwards, but as this book is not intended for people who ski backwards, let's not complicate matters with irrelevant side issues. Oh yes! It can be done and is for instance done by skiers and teachers who want to watch what is happening to following pupils and of course by people who just want to show-off, which may also include skiing teachers.

When you are moving, the force you can use to turn your skis is a product of your weight exerted through your heels multiplied by the length of the "lever" measured from the pivot point to the central point of your weight. Whereas when you are stopped, you lose the lever that produces your turning force and you can only turn by rotating your ski boots and that I hope explains why it is easier to make a turn while you are moving on your skis so as to produce a lever, rather than when you are stopped.

As long as you are on the level or on a fairly gentle slope, the faster you go the more you will increase the length of the lever or distance between your heel through which you are applying your weight and the pivot point. The longer the lever, the greater will be the force to turn your skis created by the pressure applied through your heels, to change the direction you are going. So in principle if by increasing your speed until you double the length of the lever, then you will double the turning force and of course that will make turning easier, or alternatively, when the length of the lever is doubled then the weight or pressure needed to turn your skis can in theory be halved, or anyway reduced.

Now when the pivot point moves beyond the tips of your skis, that's when it again becomes tricky. When making snow-plough or Stem Christy turns, providing you are in control of your skis, you will not be going very fast, or at least not fast enough for the pivot point to move beyond the tips of your skis. But as we are about to move on to parallel turns, which will allow you to ski a lot faster, this is when I think knowing about how the pivot point moves will help you.

After parallel turns, we will then be moving onto mogul fields when you will be skiing up or down over moguls, so your skis will be pointing up or downwards, and then you will need to know how that effects the movement of the pivot, and how this movement of the pivot point also effects your skiing.

Because the pivotal point moves further ahead of your skis as your speed increases, it will make the turning lever longer. Unfortunately when the pivot point moves beyond the tips of your skis, your skis then have to start moving sideways a lot to turn at the pivot point. Or in other words, if the pivot point moves ahead of your ski tips then by the simple laws of mechanics, it means that to make a turn rotating at the pivot point, as indicated by the spoke and the hub of the wheel, you must slide your skis sideways. This is fine if you wish to show off your long gentle curving or carving turn technique. On the other hand if you want to make a quick turn, which is more usually the case, then it is better if you have the pivot point relatively close to your ski tips. If you want, you can overcome this problem by using brute force to make a turn other than at the pivot point, but obviously it is going to make skiing a lot more strenuous and more difficult to stay in control of your skis, especially for learners, however there is an alternative way which we can use to alter the position of the pivot point.

How to alter the position of the pivot point

Fortunately there are ways by which you can alter the amount the pivot point moves to where you want it, when you are skiing. If an aeroplane or glider banks, or if a skier leans into the turn, it will reduce the amount the pivotal point moves ahead, which will shorten the length of the turning lever, or you might say it brings the pivot point nearer to your ski boots and so it will reduce the amount you will need to slide your skis sideways to make your turn.

Aircraft also slide sideways as they turn. Ships unfortunately for them can't quite do the same thing, although they can and do slide sideways, but because of the water resistance, it causes them to heel over away from the turn, which to some extent restrains them from moving sideways and causes them to require more force to make the turn. Due to the slight friction between your skis and the snow, your skis will move sideways relatively less for the same amount of pressure to make a turn than aircraft, but more than for ships.

As ships tend to heel over "away" from the turn it doesn't help them to turn at all and it won't help you either if you were to lean outwards. Speed boats with V shaped hulls can "be made" to lean into the turn to make them more manoeuvrable, and you will also need to lean into the turn like aeroplanes and gliders as well as speed boats to make a quick turn. To be more manoeuvrable, the need to slide sideways if you want to make a quick turn doesn't help you, but if you edge your skis and lean into the turn, you can bring the pivotal point back towards the skis' tips to reduce the length of the turning lever and reduce or almost remove the need for you to slide your heels sideways to turn round at the pivot point. Well! that's OK for when you are on the level or on a gentle slope, but when it gets steeper we find we have a further complication.

Going back to our ships again, (*the same also applies to aeroplanes and balloons, however for simplicity, in this case we will stick to ships,*) the pivot point will "not" move so far ahead if a ship is "not" on a level keel but is trimmed deeper at the stern so that it's bow is pointing upwards or for that matter if it is trimmed with it's bow deeper and is pointing downwards, when the pivot point will not move so far ahead relative to it's speed. Because the pivot point has not moved so far ahead of the ship, it will also not have to slip sideways so much to make a turn, even if it is not leaning into the turn, and the same thing applies to your skis. If your skis are moving uphill, such as when they go up a mogul or a hump of snow, or if they are moving down a mogul or even down a steeper piste, then the pivot point will not move so far ahead. The steeper the incline, up or down, the less the pivot point will move ahead, until they can reach a point at which the pivot point is inside your ski boot. Should you come to a stop with your skis pointing uphill, your pivotal point may even move to a position behind your ski boots, in which case you will have to either rotate your skis to point in a direction that is level or climb up or slide down to a level position, before you can move again.

When you want to make a turn or manoeuvre, the things you need to bear in mind are how far ahead the pivot point will move depends on how fast you are skiing, whether your skis are on the level or pointing up or down hill, and whether and how much you are leaning into the turn. Normally it will be a combination of all these things and will be changing all the time you are moving. Ah! But the difference now is that you will be one of those skiers who actually knows the reason why, and with experience, once you have got the feel of how your skis behave, it should all become natural to you to understand what is happening when something goes wrong.

That's about the best way that I can think of to explain how the pivot point moves and how it effects your skiing, so that you can understand why your skis behave the way they do. I don't know why the pivot point moves the way it does, I haven't ever seen or heard of any explanation, but I can assure you in reality and from experience, that is in fact how the pivot point moves, whether you are on skis, a ship or an aeroplane.

10 PARALLEL TURNS. WEDELING

The parallel turn.

The ultimate ambition for holiday skiers is to be able to make parallel turns, so as to be able to ski faster. Making parallel turns is all about arranging the distribution of your weight, and getting your balance correct.

In fact, the reason that beginners learning to ski should start with the snowplough and progress via the Stem Christy, to parallel turns, is simply because of the progressive difficulty incurred in staying in control of your skis, and keeping your balance by getting your stance and the distribution of your weight right, all at the same time. In other words, you can't get away so easily with your weight being incorrectly distributed or with a poor technique, causing you to be off-balance when doing parallel turns so much as you can while doing a snowplough or even Stem Christy turns. In return, as you progress from snowplough turns, via the Stem Christy to parallel turns, you are rewarded by being more in control of your skis as well as it being less arduous for you, while you can also ski faster, and that means it is also physically less strenuous.

I've heard people say that they started skiing straight off doing parallel turns. Maybe they did, but then I imagine that they would not be the sort of skier who would need to read this book. There will always be times when it will be sensible to use a snowplough so as to be able to keep in control of your skis, for instance if you are in a crowded area, such as in a queue and there is not enough room in which to stop other than by using a snowplough. To be perfectly frank there is no reason at all to be ashamed of using the snowplough any time you want, whether it is the most appropriate manoeuvre to use, or not.

How to make a Parallel turn.

To make your first attempt at doing a parallel turn, as you would expect you should start on a gentle slope, use the nursery slope if necessary, so that you can set off down the fall line-line without going too fast. First, assume the general stance making sure you are leaning well forward, keeping your knees bent and together, now start skiing, you need to be doing 6-7 m.p.h at least so that the pivot point has moved ahead enough, towards the tips of your skis, a bit more than a fast walking pace.

To turn to the left, you need to unweight your left ski by lowering your right buttock to lower your body weight down onto the inside of your right heel to transfer your weight onto your right ski so that you can push the tail of your skis out to your right, all at the same time, so as to make your turn to your left (*which will also change the tilt of your hips into the correct position for the new direction you will be heading relative to the fall line*) and bend your left knee more to be sure there is no weight on it. A good exercise as a learner is to actually lift your inside ski off the ground to confirm to yourself that there is no weight on it. Keep your right knee pointing to the left into the turn and also tucked in behind your left knee, to edge your right ski to avoid catching an outside edge, as you make your turn. To keep turning, push down and outwards through your right heel, make sure your backside stays in line with the rest of your body while leaning to your left into the turn, to help you to keep the pivot point close to the tips of your skis. Keep your skis parallel as you slide or skid the tail end of both of your skis to the right, and all the time keeping your body and shoulders facing towards the fall-line and keep leaning forwards so that you can feel your shins pressing up against the tongue of your boot. Keep your weight on the inside edge of your outside ski, in this case the right ski and you will make a parallel turn to your left. And then visa versa when you want to turn to the right.

After you have turned the required amount, you can assume a traversing stance by not leaning into the turn any more or pushing down on the inside of your heel, although still leaning forward and facing towards the fall-line, and retaining more of your weight on your lower right ski by keeping your right buttock lower than the left one, keep your right knee behind your left knee and pointing towards the mountain to be sure you are edging your lower ski, to avoid catching an outside edge.

To summarise to make a parallel turn: Lower your outside buttock to transfer your weight onto your outside ski with your knees pointing into the turn to edge your skis. Keep your skis parallel while pushing your heels outwards to make the turn, lean forwards and into the turn, with your shins pressing against the tongue of your ski boots, while facing towards the fall line so that your new uphill shoulder tends to be ahead, or leading you.

It may sound complicated as you read it here but if you follow all the advice I've given, I think you should soon get to feel when it's correct. Once it feels correct and you feel comfortable without any strain on your muscles, you will have mastered doing parallel turns on a gentle slope, carry on practising while increasing your speed, which means that you will need to bend your knees and lean forwards more. With the increase in your speed, while still on a gentle slope so as to rotate your skis at the pivotal point, you will need to lean into the turn more to counter the pivot point moving further ahead of your skis due to the increase in your speed. As you gain confidence you can increase the steepness of the gradient of the piste which means your skis will be pointing more downhill, so that automatically the pivot point will "not" move forward so much and then you will not need to lean into the turn so much, or alternatively you can turn more quickly. As you increase the steepness of the gradient, keep leaning towards the fall-line more and eventually given time, you will be skiing like a natural born skier.

I am aware that I am endlessly telling you to lean forward more all the time, but if you were walking instead of skiing, your natural instinct as you walk down steeper slopes is to try to remain vertical, with your weight on the balls of your feet to keep your balance, because you expect your shoes to grip the ground. But when you are skiing, then you want your skis to slide over the snow instead of griping the ground, therefore to keep your balance you need to be leaning forwards. To confirm that you are leaning forwards you need to feel your shins pressing against the tongue of your ski boots, which means that more of your weight can be transferred onto your heels and that is why I make no apologises for feeling it is necessary to keep saying to you to lean forward more. You will find that there are lots of times when you are skiing that it is necessary to do the opposite to what you would normally do out walking, if you like, you may think of it as the "the contrarian nature of the skiing beast", just see how impressed they'll be down at the pub when you say that.

While you are skiing you might like to carve long gentle turns by not leaning into the turn or edging your outside ski so much and allowing your skis to slide over the snow sideways, using the longer lever as the pivot point moves ahead of your skis, to apply less pressure on your heel. Or you might like to make quicker parallel turns by leaning into the turn and edging your skis more, particularly your outside ski, while applying more pressure through the heel of your outside ski.

When you start skiing down steeper pistes, you will probably be going faster which means that the pivot point will move forwards further, but this will be counterbalanced by your skis pointing downwards more, causing the pivot point not to move forwards so much.

With practise and experience, you will develop a feeling when you are skiing, using your parallel turns correctly, that as you push down on the inside edge of your skis to make the turn, that you will also feel you are pushing backwards on your heels to propel yourself forwards. I am not suggesting that you should actually try to push backwards to propel yourself forwards because that is not the way it works, but that if you are leaning forwards enough and with enough weight on your heels, that is what I find it will feels like. Whereas if you feel you are pushing forwards I think it is a fair bet that you are not leaning forwards enough, with too much weight on the balls of your feet, and that you need to bend your knees more so that you can put more weight on your heels. If you don't, it is almost certain that you will lose control and either fall, or come to a stop.

Carved turns.

Alternatively, you may carve a turn by leaning a lot further over into the turn and edging your skis at something like 45° or more so as to allow the bowing of your skis, due to the broader tip and tail of your skis griping the snow more than the narrower waist of your skis were your weight is applied, to guide you round a curve. This is the true way to carve a turn. This is a good exercise to do if you are interested in slalom racing, but racing is outside my province and this book. I only mention this bowing of your skis effect to carve a turn, because to some extent it always happens when making a parallel turn, especially if you are leaning well over into the turn.

What is Wedeling?

"Wedel"(*pronounce vedel*) is a German word, meaning "to wag" as in a dog's tail. With apologises to Germany and any German speakers and also in the hope that I don't offend anyone else or even wagging dog's tails, for the benefit of English speaking people the present participle of wedel has been anglicised to "wedeling".

Basically wedeling normally consists of either a quick succession of parallel turns or possibly carving a succession of slow semicircular turns, depending on what you want to do and the space available, but either way, to be wedeling, it's essentially that you don't do any traversing in between turns, so that turns follows one another in succession.

All the time you are skiing it is necessary to keep your thinking well ahead of what your skis are doing, but even more so when you are wedeling as you must not be late or hesitate in any way, if you are going to make the smooth transition from one swing to the next, which is necessary to be wedeling.

To practise wedeling start on a gentle slope, leaning forward and bending your knees a little bit more to help you to get the correct feel. If you want to start by making a swing to the left you will need to head in a direction to the right of the fall-line. Assume the general stance, once you have started moving, lower your right buttock to unweight your left ski and lower your body weight down onto your right ski and to push outwards on the inside of your right heel, still keeping your shines leaning against the tongue of your ski boots, to start making a parallel turn to your left, keep your unwewighted ski slightly ahead of your weighted ski, (*you should now be able to lift your left ski off the ground*), at the same time point your knees to your left into the turn, to edge your right ski. To continue turning to your left, keep sliding the tail end of your skis out to the right, as you would to make a left-handed parallel turn.

As you turn in a semicircle to your left, when you judge the tips of your skis are passing the fall-line, or in other words when they start crossing from your right side to your left side, you will also need to start to change your stance to stop turning to your left and start making a turn to the right. As a rough guide, when the tips of your skis start to cross the fall-line, start lowering your left buttock to transfer your weight onto your left ski and automatically unweight your right ski, and also start leaning to your right, so that you will start your new turn as your boots cross the fall line. Swing, or if you prefer, roll your knees across to point in the opposite direction to your right, so that you can edge your left ski and push down and outwards on the inside edge of your left heel to slide the tail end of your skis out to the left, so that you will start turning to your right, much the same as you would to make to make a right handed parallel turn.

Obviously there is no line painted down the piste indicating where the fall line is so you must make a judgment. However, once you have the feel of how to wedel, you will then find you are able to wedel in any direction you may chose, as long as it is downhill, and you will not need to know where the fall line is any more. It's just that to keep it as easy and simple as possible, the only way I can explain to someone who has not got the hang of how to wedel, is to start to explain how it is done by referring to the fall line.

Each time you push down on the inside of your heel to make a turn, lean away from the direction you are pushing, towards the inside of the turn, but keep your backside in line with your body and avoid moving it from side to side, as this will reduce the amount of force you exert on the heels of your skis. Try to keep your skis parallel and close together all the time.

Once you are making successive turns to your left and right, you will have started wedeling. You need to keep your hips and the rest of your body turned towards the fall-line all the time, so as to be able to transfer your weight properly. Providing your buttocks are in the correct position you shouldn't have any problems with your hips, which as you know, move in conjunction with your buttocks.

Casually wedeling.

Keep practising to make turns to the right and left in succession as quickly as you can, transferring your weight much the same as you would when you are jogging. That is, allowing your body to just rise naturally at the end of one turn as your skis start to cross the fall line, and then fall as you lower your buttock at the start the next turn, so that you can use your body weight to push down on the inside of your heel. Do not make any attempt to increase the rise and fall of your body other than that caused naturally by the raising and lowering of your buttocks, otherwise you will lose your rhythm and you will probably stop leaning forward too.

When you get the rhythm going you will find you will get the felling that the top half of your body is moving down in roughly a straight line, with your legs and skis moving from side to side without feeling any particular strain on any of your muscles and your body rising and falling with your knees pointing into each turn to have the correct edge, while your skis are carving semicircles. When that happens you will be wedeling. All you need to do now is to fine tune your technique to keep the rhythm flowing while you progress to steeper pistes and increase your speed. Remember to lean towards the fall-line and bend your knees more as the gradient increases and do not let your backside move from side to side but keep it in line with the rest of your body, also keeping your shoulders and arms relaxed.

When to wedel

Wedeling allows you to be able to control your speed as you ski down a piste instead of just schussing down. The more you edge your skis as you push down on your heels, the more you can grip the snow as you carve each turn on each swing which you can use to control of your speed, you may also help to reduce your speed by transferring a bit of your weight to push down on the balls of your feet so long as you don't reduce the amount you are leaning forward. Once you have got a natural rhythm to your wedeling, you can practise wedeling anywhere where you need to keep a tight control of your speed, rather than being reduced to side slipping or even snow ploughing, but it comes into it's own down a narrow piste or even down a path if you are really good at wedeling. Anyway as it looks more stylish, it will give you a chance to show off, providing of cause you don't fall, and if you do fall don't worry as it will give anyone watching you a laugh instead, so you see, every cloud has a silver lining.

11 MOGULS

Now, finally we come to the biggest challenge of all for piste bashers, how to ski down a mogul field?

As a guide in this context as to what constitutes a mogul field, it is an area with a succession of moguls without letup, so I am not referring to the intermittent hump and bump that you might find on any normal piste, nor am I even referring to the odd area with just half a dozen humps in succession, although they will be handy or even necessary, for you to practise on. I am thinking more of an area covered in moguls which can not be avoided, where you will need to make something like half a dozen turns over humps and bumps to get across them, and that would be the very smallest mogul field, I can assure you once you see a mogul field, as opposed to the normal piste, you will be in no doubt in recognizing that it is a mogul field. Of course there is no reason why you should not practise the manoeuvres explained in this chapter on any single mogul, where ever you are, without venturing onto a mogul field.

When skiing down mogul fields, the big difference to skiing down a piste is that normally there is not a lot of room to make your turns, on, over, or round a mogul, which means you will need to be a lot more agile, so that you are able to move more quickly. If that doesn't sound very easy, frankly that's because it's not. You will need to be prepared to do a lot of work practising to develop your mogul skiing skills so as to build up your confidence to make your turns unhesitatingly. However, most skiers are able scramble down a mogul field more or less coming to a stop after each turn and probably in between them too, so as long as you are not tired there is no reason why you shouldn't try, but what you need to be aiming for is to be able to ski down a mogul field competently, which means being able to continue skiing, making as many turns as and were you feel like making them and going as far as you wish without stopping. When you are able to do that, you will find that skiing down moguls also becomes a lot less strenuous for you and therefore more fun.

The most common mistake when skiing down mogul fields is not to lean forwards enough or keeping your knees together or reasonably close together, which is probably because you keep meeting the face of the upward slope of the next mogul, which will tend to throw you backwards, not something you would normally expect to encounter down ordinary pistes. To overcome this you need to bend your knees more, and force yourself to keep leaning forwards, so that you are pressing your shins against the tongue of your ski boots while also keeping your shoulders relaxed. To help you to carry your weight forwards as you ski up the face of a mogul, you might like to try giving your arms a little forwards swing and even slightly raise your body to increase your momentum, and then you should be alright.

When skiing down a mogul field you will be working continuously to correct your stance by the raising and lowering of your buttocks, which will adjust the attitude of your hips as you keep transferring your weight onto your lower ski. As a general rule it works out that you will normally be transferring your weight from one ski to the other at the bottom of the valley between the moguls, rolling your knees from side to side, as required to keep them pointing into the mountain to edge your skis correctly, and continually facing towards the fall line, which means that you will be leading with your uphill shoulder. As long as you are in general facing down the fall line of the whole mogul field, while continuously moving your buttocks to keep your weight on your lower ski, then you should find that your hips will automatically be facing in the required direction.

Down steeper slopes the sides of the moguls are more likely to be steeper, in which case not only must you force yourself to bend your knees and lean forwards but it will also be necessary to increase the effort you put into your skiing by exaggerating or if you prefer, increasing the rising and falling of your buttocks to be able push down with your body weight. When you come to think about it, it is only logical that steeper mogul fields will be more difficult to ski down and therefore it is going to require more effort. Once you have learnt to handle skiing down mogul fields and got the feel of it, it will become more natural, and skiing them easier. Well again! That's the theory

To be honest, lots of people never even try to ski down mogul fields, or if they do, it will only be when they have to, and as I have already mentioned most skiers are able scramble down a mogul field. On the other hand, if you are already reasonably competent at doing parallel turns, then you should have that feel that will make sure you have your weight properly distributed on your lower skis, and that you are leaning forwards, pressing against the tongue of your ski boot to ski comfortably. In other words, you should have reached the stage when you can feel if you are making your turns correctly or not. Skiing is like almost any sport, when you do it right, it feels right. Well that's been my guide for the past forty odd years or so, although I have to admit it's more often to let me know that I'm not doing it right rather than the occasional ecstatic feeling I get when it's letting me know that I've got it right at last, therefore I don't see why it shouldn't work for you too.

You can start learning to handle moguls on the odd individual moguls you will find on any piste, unless they have been groomed out of existence, never mind, I'm sure there are bound to be moguls on other pistes and most resorts will have areas of moguls scattered around the red if not the blue pistes that you can practice on.

Skiing down mogul fields will require all the skills you have already learnt, I am not trying to suggest that you need to be completely and fully competent at all the skiing skills to tackle a mogul field, but I would suggest that without being able to manage a decent parallel turn then you are going to find it hard work on anything other than the easiest mogul fields. Obviously the steeper the mogul field, the more difficult it is to ski down and therefore will require greater competence. I've seen skiers, whom I presume have made a mistake and got onto the wrong piste, trying to snowplough down mogul fields between the mogul peaks, but it looks like hard work and invariably they frequently fall, which can't be a lot of fun or help their confidence, which must make it even worse for them. I'm afraid on steeper mogul fields it is more likely that the gullies or valleys between the peaks, will be so deep that there will not be enough room for it to be possible to snowplough between the peaks.

Mogul fields vary according to how steep the slope is and how they have been developed depending on the prevailing weather conditions, and how much they have been skied. Early in the season when the days are short, and the weather is more likely to be consistently cold, the mogul fields on gentle slopes will tend to simply be heaps of snow scattered about in a fairly regular pattern, later in the season when "spring snow" is more common, the valleys between the moguls tend to get carved out more, making them deeper and the peaks tend to get joined up and develop into ridges. On steeper mogul fields no matter what the time of the season it is, the sides of the moguls will also be steeper and the peaks will tend to be joined, so that instead of simple peaks you will have irregular shaped ridges, again, if the mogul field is popular with good aggressive skiers, they will tend to carve out the valleys between the peaks even deeper.

Ideally, to learn to ski moguls, start on the odd moguls that you will normally find on any piste as explained below. Try turning on their peaks first, and when you can do that, try skiing round the peaks with your weight on your lower ski, and when you think you have learnt to do that, you can go for the big one, turning on the face of the mogul. After that you can start learning to ski down whole mogul fields, on as gentle slopes as you can find and with practise you will be able to increase the gradient of the slope until you can tackle steeper slopes with ridges. You will then have to make your turn as you ski over the top of the ridge instead of turning around peaks, that is, until you have learnt to turn on the face of the mogul. All the time you will still have to distribute your weight using more or less the same techniques you have already learnt, it's just that as you are now skiing down moguls, you will need to be that little bit more careful and accurate. I'm afraid there is no easy, casual, or laid back way to ski down mogul fields.

Skiing from mogul peak to peak

The simplest way to make a turn on a mogul is first to ski up onto it's peak, but beware when you start to go up the side of the mogul it will tend to throw you backward, therefore you need to make sure that your knees are well bent and that you are leaning well forward. When you reach the top of the mogul, simply rotate your ski boots to turn towards the direction you wish to proceed and ski down. Job done! Well yes, up to a point, and if there is more than one mogul, as long as the piste is not too steep you can expect that there will be plenty of room between the moguls, so that you'll be able to ski from mogul to mogul, turning on each peak.

However that doesn't happen too often, probably the peaks will be too close together and then the valley between them will be too deep, which means that you will probably finish up stopped in the bottom of the valley, and then you will have to climb back up the mogul onto it's peak to make a fresh start, and that is very hard work. Never the less turning on the peak of moguls is a handy technique to start with.

Skiing round a mogul peak.

The next tactic is to be able to ski round the peak of a mogul. The principle is the same as making a parallel turn but round the peak, however, this will be more difficult because your outside ski with your weight on, will be a lot lower than your inside unweighted ski. As you need to have your weight on your outside ski, it therefore means that you will need to lower your outside buttock and also bend your inside knee a lot more than if you were making a ordinary parallel turn on the level, however, it will make sure that your hips are at the correct angle to lean towards the fall line, as well as into the turn. What with having to lean well forward as you ski up the mogul and then lowering your buttock more than normal to make the turn, it will require a lot more agility and energy than making a normal turn on the piste, which will make it more strenuous.

When you lean forward to ski up the side of a mogul, as you reach the top, if you "don't" want to loose any speed and to keep your momentum going, roll your skis over the top of the mogul. On the other hand, if you want to loose some momentum and check your speed, then delay rolling your skis over the top of the mogul by allowing a bit more of your weight onto the balls of your feet for a fraction of a second, but don't overdo it or you may come to a stop and then slide backwards down the mogul into the valley, after practising it a few times, I think you should soon get the hang of it.

Skiing around the peaks of moguls will get you down a mogul field but it ain't 'alf hard work, which may account for some skiers not being too keen on skiing down moguls, so I expect that you'll soon be looking for an easier technique, which will be to make your turns on the face of the mogul.

Turning on the face of a mogul

The main thing about turning on the face of a mogul is that it will require more skill, agility and good timing to be successful. There are basically two ways to turn on the face of a mogul using either the normal parallel turn, or alternatively, an "unwieghting turn" which is explained below.

If the mogul is small or shallow and/or you are not going fast enough to achieve enough unweighting force or lift to make a turn, then you should be able to make a normal parallel turn by lowering your outside buttock, so long as you make sure you get your timing right. If you turn too early you will not reach the face of the mogul, or if you leave it too late then you will be on the mogul peak or you may even fly over the top of the mogul. In other words you must not hesitate and be precise, so as to turn on your chosen spot on the face of the mogul, if you manage to do that then the principles are the same as doing any other parallel turn. Remember to keep leaning forwards as well as into the turn.

Note that as you approach the turn and again as you leave after making your turn, your lower ski with your weight on will be the same ski, even though you will have needed to transfer your weight onto your upper ski by lowering your outside buttock for a short time to push outwards to make the turn, and that will be a good test of your agility.

Unweighted turn

To make an "unweighted turn" you will require a new technique. You will need to ski up the face of a larger mogul, or for that matter the face of any other slope of solid snow *(as opposed to soft snow, when your ski tips might simply go straight into the snow)*, at a sufficient speed to create a force that will want to throw or tip you over backwards. To counter this force as you start to ski up the face of the mogul or slope, you will also need to create an opposing force by launching or throwing yourself forwards, swinging your arms forwards and slightly raising your body at the same time will help to add extra momentum. The result of combining these two forces, you throwing yourself forwards and raising your body, and the mogul tipping you over backwards, is to create an unweighting or an uplifting force, which will be enough to unweight the tail of your skis, so that you can rotate your body, in the same way as you can jump up and turn in the air in your front room, to make as much of a turn as you require before your weight returns onto your skis, to enable you to ski down the face of the mogul in your required new direction. Maybe it will help you, if you think of your legs as springs that are being compressed by these two forces as you ski up the mogul face, and then the forces can be released to unweight your skis. You must make sure your timing is correct, as if you start to launch yourself forward too soon the force will dissipate before it combines with the force tipping you over backwards, probably leaving you stranded or coming to a stop or actually falling down backwards, and if it is done too late, you could finish up trying to make a jump, which is OK if you succeed but makes it a lot harder work, and if you don't succeed then you will fall down or possibly fly over the top of the mogul before falling down. Therefore starting to launch yourself forwards as you start your ascent up the face of the mogul is crucial. It is not difficult as long as you are confident in what you are doing, then it shouldn't really cause you any problems. Again your weight will be on the same ski as you go up and on your way down, but at least you don't have to transfer any weight onto your uphill ski. This may sound difficult to do, but is not really so difficult if you can do parallel turns competently, and as long as you are fully committed.

The more agile skiers will be able to ski immediately from face to face until they reach their destination, but for beginners, you can simply weave your way between the moguls until you are fully composed to ski up the face of a mogul to make your next turn, and it will still get you down without requiring too much effort. It just means that you will need a bit more time and a wider mogul piste.

Once you have got the hang of turning on the face of moguls you won't want to use any other way, much the same as when you have learnt to do parallel turns you will more or less discard habitually using the Snowplough and Stem Christy turns, but until then, you will probably start by using a combination of turning on peaks, around peaks and eventually on the face of moguls to get down mogul fields.

If you are lucky enough to find a "half pipe" in the snow, as used by snow boarders, then you will have the chance to show off a bit by crisscrossing your way down the half pipe, using the same unweighting technique to make your turns. With a bit more effort you will be able to get completely air-bourn as you reach the top of the side of the half pipe, so that you can hopefully make a spectacular turn in the air, at least in your estimation, before skiing back down the side of the half pipe again and up the other side. As is my luck when I thought I would show off, I had to stop half way down the half pipe to let someone innocently snow ploughing down the middle of the half pipe to pass, and sure enough when it was clear, so help me if all of my audience hadn't gone too, as if life isn't already difficult enough for us old timers.

Mogul fields.

Steeper mogul fields tend to be made up of tracks of deep valleys, criss-crossing the mogul field making a succession of humps and bumps between them, whether you are skiing to your left or right. If you get on a steep mogul field like this you will soon see what I mean. You will probably get the feeling that the tracks are too narrow to have enough room to make a turn without the tail end of your skis hitting the uphill side of the valley, which causes you to keep hesitating to make a turn. Consequently you finish up skiing along the track crossing the whole mogul field from one side to the other, which will help to deepen the tracks, and only making a turn when you are forced to at the end of each track. Because you are not attacking the moguls, but instead, the moguls are throwing you around, this will become strenuous work, and tiring as you ski up and down over the humps and bumps along the tracks, not to mention that you will only make a little progress down the mogul field. It's my guess that it's because so many skiers keep hesitating to make a turn as they ski back and forth, criss-crossing the mogul field from one side to the other, that this is how you finish up with these tracks. In fact if you do make a turn there will always be sufficient room for the tail end of your skis on the uphill side of the mountain, therefore, it means you can completely ignore the feeling that there isn't enough room, and go ahead and make your turn.

As you ski down a mogul field it is much better to try to make a steady succession of turns without stopping, so that you can maintain enough speed to have your pivot point where you want it, somewhere between just ahead of your boots and at the most not more than a foot or two ahead of your ski tips, and then you will make good progress and not tire yourself out. Believe me you will normally make as much progress doing three or four turns downhill, as you would crossing the whole mogul field, and in the end it is the easiest way to get down. So, to give yourself confidence, you just need to convince yourself that you can do it, or resign yourself to a lot of hard work and getting tired.

While you are learning, you will certainly not be going fast enough for the pivotal point to move too far ahead of the tips of your skis when skiing down mogul fields. Also, as you ascend or descend moguls, your skis will be pointing either up or downwards quite steeply, which will bring the pivot point right back inside your ski boots (*5° to 10° is more than enough*), or worse still behind your ski boots if you are too slow, and remove any turning lever altogether, which will really make it difficult to make a turn. That means that if you don't maintain enough momentum you could end up stopped, and stranded in the bottom of a valley between moguls, and left to struggle up to the top of the next mogul before you can carry on. Therefore it is essential to develop your mogul skiing skills, to maintain enough momentum to keep the pivot point ahead of your ski boots, so that it is not too strenuous work.

Don't try to learn to ski down steep mogul fields when your legs are feeling tired because you won't learn anything at all, come back when you are feeling bright eyed and bushy tailed. When you have become proficient at doing all the skills mentioned so far, you will have learnt to be able to turn on the sides of moguls, as well as on the ridges, side slipping down one mogul and skiing up the side of another, when you can do all that, then you will be able to call yourself a good piste bashing mogul skier. In fact I think you will deserve a medal.

I have one more gem of information for you regarding mogul fields, when standing at the top of a mogul field looking around, trying to decide whether it is a good day for you to tackle moguls, it will appear that the moguls are not so big or steep the further away they are either to your left or right, compared to those you see when facing down the fall line. This is an allusion caused by the different aspect or angle from which you are looking at them, you see the nearer you are to the moguls the more you are looking down on them. Whereas the moguls on the same level as you which are farther away, will be viewed from a more horizontal direction, and therefore will look flatter and not so steep. So when deciding whether to tackle a particular mogul run, don't be deceived into thinking that by skiing to the other side of the mogul field that you will find that it is easier over there, because when you get there, you will find that they are just as steep, but by then you will be committed to going to the bottom of the mogul field, or possibly having an even harder struggle climbing back to where you started. As always when skiing, you must be positive but especially when skiing mogul fields, as with any hesitation it will be too late. As they say now-a-days, you must "go for it", especially if the moguls are steep and close together, which will make skiing them even more difficult, and that I think is the ultimate challenge for the piste bashing holiday skier.

12 MISCELLANEOUS INFORMATION. SKIING CONDITIONS AND EXPERIENCES

Climbing uphill on skis.

From time to time you will want to climb uphill without having to take off your skis, there are basically four different ways of doing this.

The easiest way is to simply walk uphill, but of course this is only possible on very gentle slopes, anything steeper and you will slide backwards, putting your ski -poles in the snow behind you to push on to stop you from sliding backwards will help and allow you to climb up slightly steeper slopes

As a matter of interest, for walking across country, "skins" so called because I think they were originally made from seal skins but now-a-days are normally made from man made fibre materials, can be fitted to the soles of your skis with the fur laid backwards, so that the skis will slide forwards easily but grip in the snow to stop you from sliding backwards, to allow you to walk up hill, but skins are for cross country skiing, and are not normally available to the holiday piste basher.

Another way of walking uphill is by the means of the herring bone walk, this requires you to face uphill and put your ski poles in the snow behind you to lean on. Put your skis in a V shape with the heels of the skis together and the points wide apart, you might describe it as the reverse of the snow plough position, with the ski toes or tips pointing uphill. By closing your knees to turn your skis onto their inside edges to get a better grip of the snow, will allow you to walk up slightly steeper hills than straight walking uphill, in practise I find I tend to use the herring bone walk after straight walking gets too steep, so it is simply a matter of opening your ski toes and keeping your knees close together to edge your skis, to change from walking to herring bone walking. I would suggest you make your first attempt at herringbone walking on nearly flat snow to get the feel of it. It will require a lot more effort.

The most useful means of climbing uphill on steeper slopes is to side step, which is done simply by standing at right angles to the fall-line with your weight on your lower ski. Lift your upper ski and place it as far uphill as you can comfortably, then lower your uphill buttock to raise your body and transfer your weight onto your upper ski to lift yourself uphill, while lifting your lower ski and place it back alongside your upper ski, you will now have progressed a short distance uphill, repeat as often as is required to reach your destination. The advantages of this method are that you can climb up any steep snow covered slopes and although it requires a lot of effort, it does not require much skill.

Now we come to the impressive or stylish way of climbing uphill. First you start with the herringbone walk, but instead of plodding from one step to the next, you start using a skating action, when for example you place your right ski on the snow, and start sliding it forward by pushing away from your weighted left ski and possibly pushing backwards on your ski poles too to help, as you glide forward and upwards, now you have to transfer your weight onto right ski. Picking up your left ski that you have just pushed away from, and when placing it at an angle to your right ski that you are sliding on, transferring your weight onto left as you push away from your right ski again, to carry on gliding forwards and uphill, and so on like skating. To skate uphill also requires a lot of effort, however it can become useful for moving along flattish snow, or even down hill if the snow is wet and sticky, so give it a go as you never know when it will come in handy. It also looks more impressive than walking, if you are in the mood to show-off a bit. Oh yes! Skiers are well known for doing a lot of showing off.

When you get up, we will join our friends over there.

Getting your thoughts together

For the absolute beginner or someone reading this book who may be just contemplating whether to try skiing will be by now wondering how can you remember to do all these different things at the same time, other than by carrying this book in your pocket? Well! Forget the multi-taskers, the fact is that you can only think of one thing at any one moment, everything else you wish to think of will be peripheral to that one thought. However, you will have a good chance of recalling anything that is available peripherally or if you prefer in your sub-conscience, if you have only just been thinking about it, in fact after a little experience, you will almost certainly carry out all the things in your subconscious without any further thought. You do it all the time, driving the car, talking and making notes or eating at the same time, these are all things you have learnt to do without thinking, O.K. I accept you don't have to learn to eat, but if you are drinking, then at least when you were a toddler, you had to learn how to hold the cup. So when you are starting to learn to ski, what you have to do is think of all the things you want to remember before you start to do an exercise or in other words, gather your thoughts together, so first of all you might start by thinking of all the things you need for the general stance, then you might add that you intend to make a turn to your left or right at such and such point, and run through in your mind how you intend to execute the turn, that should be enough for a start. Getting into the general stance you can do before you start to move and it will still be in the periphery of your mind, now think how you are going to execute the turn by changing your stance and shifting your weight while facing towards the fall-line and then off you go, only thinking of where you are going to make your turn and relying on recalling the thoughts in the periphery of your mind to get you round. With practice the next thing you know, you will be able to do the turn without having to think about it at all as now it will all be entrenched in your sub-conscience and will have become second nature to you.

A brief introduction to ski lifts

First there are T-bars and button drag lifts. Buttons are used singly and placed between your legs onto your bottom to drag you up a track. T-bars are for pairs and are placed between two skiers with each side of the T bar on their bottom to drag them up a track, if you are on your own and there is no one else to join you on the T-bar, then you will have to go up on your own, it is not obligatory to go in twos. When you first see them you will find it is pretty obvious how to use them.

Next we come to chair lifts (*almost like bench settees, although occasionally you may come across an old single chair lift*) which can take from just one to anything up to eight skiers at a time, and I am told there are even more seaters, but eight is the most I have seen, and they are carried up the mountain on a continuous cable strung over pylons. Normally skiers sit side by side facing up the mountain, but I've been on one where the chair travelled sideways. Again when you see them it is obvious how they operate. Some of the latest chairs move slowly to pick up the skiers before speeding off up the mountain, they will also slow down again at the top to let you off, while the less sophisticated ones just continue at the same speed all the time, with these I advise you to put your hand on the edge of the chair as you are about to sit down, to stop it from hitting the back of your legs, if not, after the first half dozen times it starts to hurt.

There should be a supervisor to see you on and off chairlifts, although there may not always be one to see you off buttons and T bars

Finally we come to cable cars and gondolas, which are boxes or carriages in which you either stand up in or there are seats to sit on, which can be as small as two seater gondolas, to cable cars sometimes carrying more than a hundred skiers at a time.

Off piste

The next thing is skiing off-piste. Skiing off-piste is not particularly more difficult than piste bashing and is certainly not so difficult as skiing down a steep mogul field, if you can ski down the piste in new snow or when it is actually snowing, competently, you shouldn't have any trouble skiing off-piste. Of course skiing off-piste allows you to go to other places. Going to other places maybe interesting but can also be more difficult or even dangerous, which again can give you more thrills because you don't know what to expect and then again, if you are not familiar with the area, you may finish up with one thrill too many. Not that I am trying to put anyone off skiing "off piste", it just depends what you want out of skiing, but it is worth bearing it in mind. If you want to practise skiing "off piste" it's better not to go very far off piste "on your own", is would be better if you where to find someone who is an experienced off-piste skier to go with. Maybe you might like to bear in mind that two inexperienced fools skiing off piste on their own are no wiser than one fool and probably twice as dangerous.

Incidentally it might be a good idea to check your insurance, some insurance policies don't cover you for skiing off-piste.

Well! This is about as far as I can take you. If you wish to go further you will need to go out and buy a more advanced skiing book, or seek help elsewhere or find a restaurant on a more difficult skiing area so that you can learn from watching better skiers while you enjoy the sun and the beer. Good luck! The choice is all yours.

The weather. Visibility and difficult conditions.

Weather conditions play a major part in skiing, other than the effect that it has on your enjoyment and comfort.

To start with, "visibility" is especially important and makes a big difference to your skiing. If it is a bright sunny day, then you can see all the humps, bumps and indentations and although you may not realise it, your brain takes in all the information and uses it to prepare you to get your timing and skiing stance right, so that you are able to make turns and keep your balance. If you learn to do a certain operation in good visibility, believe me, even if it is only overcast the next time you try to repeat the same operation, it is quite likely you will have a lot more difficulty doing it.

After a good day's skiing on a lovely bright sunny day, you will return to your lodgings absolutely delighted with yourself, proudly telling everyone who may be interested, how well you have done and why not? Then the next day you go out and the weather is miserable, it's overcast, you have a terrible time trying to ski, you lose confidence in your skiing and nothing goes right, you are falling down all over the place and you don't know why, you return to your lodgings, and what do you find, everyone else has been having exactly the same problems, simply because of the poorer visibility, believe me, that's all it takes when you start learning to ski but don't be disheartened, because with practise and experience, you are going to learn to conquer all conditions.

Bearing in mind that this book is aimed mainly at beginners, especially adult beginners, as well as the enthusiastic skiers with problems, I wish to draw your attention to being aware that as the day wares on your muscles will be tiring and the temptation is to become lazy and not put as much effort into your skiing as you should. This is a big mistake to make! What actually happens is that your lazy skiing makes it more strenuous for you and consequently it tires you even more quickly. The proper reaction to feeling tired is to concentrate more on skiing correctly, which will make it less work for you, and then probably take a break, or possibly, if it is at the end of the day, go for the easiest route back home, maybe even after also taking a break.

Now to add to your difficulties it starts to snow and in no time it is 2-3 cms or ½" deep. Suddenly it is like skiing off piste and your skis seem to be catching outside edges, or at least that is what it feels like, for no apparent reason you keep falling and it's very frustrating because you don't understand why, again it's mainly because of the bad visibility, you now have absolutely no idea of where the bumps and dips are, and in the new snow which quite possibly is also wet and sticky, even the slightest error in your skiing will unbalance you.

With these conditions you basically have two options, to give up and retreat to the nearest hostelry in the hope of some libation and warmth until conditions get better. Or alternatively you may think that to be a proper skier, you have to learn to ski in all conditions and quite right too. However, if you are an absolute beginner, other than if you are practising on the nursery slopes, I hope you do not have too far to go, because to be honest beginners will not learn anything by struggling in really difficult conditions in poor visibility in falling snow.

When the skiing gets difficult then essentially it means you must "concentrate more" on what you are doing, you might think this is pretty obvious and so it is when reading a book, but on the slopes when you are finding difficulties you are not expecting to contend with, it's all very different. This probably means that you will be feeling anxious and in consequences you are not as relaxed as you should be and as I have already mentioned, any stress for whatever reason, will introduce unwanted tension in your muscles, which will make it more difficult to ski properly as well as making it more tiring.

Now that you are relaxed and concentrating, what should you be concentrating on? The first most likely fault will be that you are not leaning forwards and as far as you can judge, facing towards the fall-line, so check that your shins are pressing up against the tongue of your ski boots. Then make sure you keep your knees bent so that you can keep more of your weight on your heels, also make sure your knees are pointing into the mountain to avoid catching an outside edge. If you can concentrate on just doing those things all at the same time, then you should be able to ski quite successfully and for beginners in difficult conditions, that will be a major achievement.

Another problem you need to be aware of in snowy, or for that matter in foggy or any other conditions which restrict your visibility, is that you will need to take care that you don't get lost. The real trouble starts if you are on an unfamiliar piste and you can't see from one piste marker to the next one. Try and make sure you stay on the piste, sometimes you can tell by stabbing the snow with your ski pole, when off the piste you can expect the snow to be softer. If you think you have left the piste it may well be worth retracing you tracks to get back onto the piste, it depends on how well you know the area, it may be worth stopping to listen for other skiers to help you to get your bearings. Unless you know it is safe to do so, such as knowing it is safe so long as you do not enter the trees or something like that, do not blunder on in the hope you will be OK, the odds are that you won't be. The logic is that if it was an area that is suitable for skiing, then there would already be a prepared piste.

Ice.

If you hit some ice then in one respect the same applies as when it's snowing, "more concentration", because your skis will slide a lot quicker over ice. Particularly make sure that you are bending your knees as you lean forwards so as to make sure you have more of your weight on your heels and that you are facing down towards the fall-line, an then concentrate on making sure your skis are edged properly, especially if it's black ice. To do that, make sure that your knees are pointed into the mountain and you are pushing down hard through the inside edge of your ski-boot, so that your ski edge gets as good a grip of the ice as possible.

Spring snow.

Spring snow is really a pseudonym for slush but slush doesn't sell so well, so spring snow it is. The problem with spring snow is that skis tend to stick in it. Normally beginners think it's terrific because then their skis don't slide away from underneath them so easily, which means they don't fall down so much, so for the absolute beginners, look for the spring snow and to heck with your instructor's whinging. If you are doing Stem Christy turns or better, you will probably prefer to avoid spring snow if you can, so in that case go higher up the mountain, where the snow should be better.

Putting wax on your skis will help them to slide over the spring snow, I still carry a block of the old silver wax with me to rub onto the soles of my skis if required, I understand the modern equivalent is wax in a spray can. It is a mistake to think that as wax allows your skis to run smoothly and faster, it will make skiing more difficult, it's because spring snow stops your skis from running smoothly that it makes your skiing difficult. So never hesitate to wax your skis in spring snow, even for beginners, especially if it is really slushy even though modern ski soles don't stick in spring snow so much as the skis we had in years gone by, I'm sure they will still benefit from some wax, anyway one thing's for sure, it won't do any harm.

The best ways to avoid spring snow is to book your holiday between December and February, when the sun is at it's lowest, or choose a skiing resort at a high altitude where it will be colder, although the higher resort will probably cost you more. But what ever you do, at the end of the day there is still no guarantee that it will not turn warm and give you spring snow, although it will be a lot less likely to in high resorts or in mid winter than in lower resorts or in the spring time.

Finally if in spite of taking all precautions, the weather turns warm and you want to avoid the spring snow, then I would suggest that you should start as early as you can or when the lifts start in the morning, before the sun starts warming up the air and turning the snow to slush, on the other hand if it has been freezing during the night, then your problem may well be ice and the solution maybe either to find a north facing slope or going higher up the mountain to look for snow that hasn't melted the day before and then frozen over into ice during the night. Or you can wait for the sun to thaw the ice but then it might turn straight back to slush again. Yes well, there's a tricky one.

A real danger with spring snow is that the skiing conditions on the piste will be variable, or in other words it will be slushier in the parts where it is in the sunshine than in the parts where it is in the shade. That means that your skis will run better in the shady parts and will not run well in the slushy sunny parts, sometimes when the sun has been shining, by the afternoon when going from good snow in the shade, into a sunny part of the piste where the snow has turned into slush, as you hit the slush it feels as though your skis have hit a brick wall. I'm not joking, it can be as bad as that. If you are aware that you are about to hit slush, stop leaning forward so much, or even not at all if you judge it to be really bad and be prepared for your body to be thrown forwards, maybe violently, the moment you hit the slush. This is the time I mentioned at the beginning of this book, which is the exception to the rule that you must always lean forwards, that is, apart from off-piste skiing which is outside the realms of this book.

Another problem caused by sunny days is that the sun melts the surface of the snow and then when the sun goes down freezes over, forming a crust on top of the snow by the next morning, which of course is known as crusted snow. It will depend on how strong the crust is but you may be skiing along quite happily on the hard snow not even aware that it is a crust. All of a sudden the crust gives way and you fall through, your skis disappear underneath the crust, a bit of panic, then as you are still moving forwards your ankles hit the edge of the broken crust and you are thrown off balance and you fall down head first. Your face hits the crust maybe causing lots of small cuts, and there speaks the voice of experience.

Well! I think in general terms, that about covers the difficult conditions. I suppose I could be more specific covering all sorts of different conditions, in fact I guess it is possible for someone to write a whole book on the subject, but not me.

Significant revelations.

I thought I would say a few words about some of the skiing revelations I have experienced, all of which happened after I stopped attending ski school, as I think you might find them interesting, as they helped me to improve my skiing techniques.

One day, as I was skiing down a steepish section of a red run and I was thinking to myself that if I could make quicker turns then I would need less space, which would help me to be able to ski more competently down a steep piste. Consequently I then thought to myself, if instead of going through all the preparations I had been taught to do in ski school to transfer my weight in readiness to make a turn, what would happen if I simply pressed down on my uphill ski in exactly the same way as you do out walking to transfer your weight? So that's what I tried and was amazed at the speed at which I spun round. Whow! I thought how much easier is that, let's forget that I almost fell down, so after that experience, after a little practise, that's the technique I adopted for transferring my weight onto my uphill ski to make a turn. By making quicker turns the advantages are that you don't need so much space to turn in, you don't spend enough time heading down the fall line to effect your speed, and of course as it is simpler and easier I found it meant that I had a better control of my skis. Hey! What more could one wish from a revelation?

But that's not all, I then noticed that it was much easier to concentrate on lowering my uphill buttock to transfer my weight quickly than it was concentrating on the position of my hips. Once I had started thinking about the movement of my buttocks, I then realised that in fact they worked in conjunction with my hips, and then it dawned on me that if my buttocks were in their correct position, then automatically my hips would also be facing in the right direction too. So, as I found it was easier to be aware of the position and movement of my buttocks than my hips, so as to keep my weight distributed correctly, I had automatically solved the problem of keeping my hips facing towards the fall line too. For me, it was probably the biggest improvement I ever made to understanding how to ski.

On a bright sunny day I was casually skiing down a piste, when I suddenly realised that I was about to joint another piste, down which I could hear other skiers coming, and ultimately I finished up having to make a quick turn to avoid a collision and let them pass. Feeling rather pleased with my quick reaction, I started thinking about how had I managed to do it, when I realised that for no reason that I was aware of, I had simply transferred more of my weight onto my heels to make a turn. Up and until that moment I had not been particularly aware, or given much thought to how or where my weight was being transferred through my boots onto my skis, but after that experience, it dawned on me that it was very important whether my weight was being transferred through my heel or the ball of my foot. So after that incident, as I set off on my way, I thought I would try transferring more of my weight onto my skis through my heels to see what, if any difference it made, and I found that in fact, I had a lot better control of my skis, this made me realise I had been transferring far too much of my weight onto my skis through the ball of my foot. At the same time I also realised that to put more weight on my heels, I could only do that by bending my knees more. From then on I gave a lot more thought to whether my weight was on my heels or the ball of my foot, to discover what difference it made to controlling my skis. I think the problem stems from the fact that normally when you walk along the road you tend to have more of your weight on the balls of your feet. Before that experience, any attempt I had made at wedeling had been a joke, but from then on I was able to start making a fairly decent attempt at wedeling. In fact I don't think it would be going too far to say that the "putting more weight on my heels" experience, was the basis for me improving my whole skiing technique.

On another occasion I was standing around on the piste taking a short break, watching other people skiing as you do, when I just happened to noticed a skier make a turn on the face of a mogul, and I thought that it looked a lot less strenuous than skiing round moguls, so then I tried to see if I could do the same and failed. However it did set me thinking about how to turn on the face of a mogul, and so I took to observing good mogul skiers and by trial and error, and with determination I was eventually able to work out how to do it, and then with practise I was able to develop my technique and build up my confidence, so that I found it to be less strenuous, which meant that eventually it became my preferred method of skiing moguls.

That I think covers my main "road to Damascus" skiing moments, although I imagine like everyone else, I am always trying out any new ideas that I might come across to improve my skiing.

The ultimate skiing conditions.

Now please indulge me while I eulogise about what I think must certainly be the ultimate skiing experience, if not the ultimate of all experiences, well it certainly was for me. First you need to find the sort of snow to die for, the really scarce, real "deep dry powder". Dry powder snow is snow that is so cold that you can not squeeze it into a snowball, because as soon as you release the pressure, it falls apart again. I experienced it for the first and only time so far, a few years ago now, but it still gives me a really gloriously satisfying glow whenever I think about it.

It was a dark stormy night in Courchevel in France, with the roar of thunder and flashes of lightning, that it snowed cats and dogs, (white ones of course) that I thought it wouldn't be possible for me to ski the next day in the new deep snow. But how wrong I was! The next morning was the start of a gorgeous day with the sun shinning out of a clear blue sky, there was not a breath of wind although it was freezing cold. All the skiers who were venturing out on the new snow covered pistes, were heading to the Verdons lift and then up the Vizelle lift, so I decided it would be sensible to follow them, at the top of the mountain the air was so cold and crisp, you could see the little particles of frozen moisture floating in the atmosphere, sparkling like small diamonds in the sunshine. Everyone was setting off down the Combe Saulire, a red run along the bottom of the valley to the right of the lift, which had collected all the new snow that had been blown into it during the storm. They were only skiing down as far as the bottom of the Vizelle lift so I followed, the snow was pure dry powder, which I would guess was at least 1.5 metres deep and it was share dream skiing, I was surprised to find that as long as I concentrated on skiing correctly, with the point of my skis slightly raised, it was not difficult. You just flowed along requiring no effort at all, with your body sailing through the deep snow as if you were floating, without leaving any tracks, just a cloud of powder snow swirling around in the air behind you. It's about as near as I have ever got to feeling like a bird gliding through the air, or what I imagine poets mean by "floating on gossamer wings", it was the most exhilarating experience I have ever known, and these conditions lasted at least for the next three days, when my holiday ended, and sadly I had to bid farewell and return home.

After that experience I started to look for more dry powder snow which took me to Canada, but unfortunately I didn't find any dry powder snow. I gathered from the locals that to have dry powder snow I would have to wait for the temperature to drop to below -20° C, which seemed a bit extreme to me, and then have a new fall of snow. I would also need a special face mask to avoid frostbite, (*I still have mine unused*) as nobody would be allowed onto the ski-lift if they had any bare skin showing. Even then it would be too cold to do more than one run, well at -20° C I suppose it would be, so it would be a case of retiring to some warm hostelry to thaw out before you could have another try. What with one thing and another, I didn't think that it was worth going all the way to Canada for dry powder snow after all. I had lasted some 30 years or more before finding dry powder in Courchevel, and it certainly didn't sound anything like my experience there. I suspect the Canadians were trying to boast their macho image by making it sound so tough, well they succeeded, not so much in boasting their image but as far as I was concerned, it sounded too tough for me to go looking for dry powder snow in Canada, certainly after my experience at Courchevel.

All I have to say now is that I hope that I have helped you to understand how to be able to ski better, and that you have enjoyed reading all my explanations and ideas on how to ski, and to wish you the best of luck, otherwise it will mean that all my efforts will have been in vain.

36334981R00055

Made in the USA
Middletown, DE
30 October 2016